Even More Wit and Wisdom of an Ordinary Subject

Malcolm Watson (signature)

Malcolm Watson

Soldier, Cricketer, Man of Letters

First published July 2023 using Kindle Direct
Publishing

First revise

ISBN 9798852716255

In memory of
Major General Jeremy Phipps, a brother
officer, who prompted a letter to the *Daily
Telegraph* and then *The Times* (page 53),
three weeks before he died on
16 March 2021.

and of

Major Bob Stapley, my driver in my first
troop in 1969, who rose through the ranks to
be commissioned in 1989 and died on
26 September 2018.

FOREWORDS

Soldier

Letter writing can be an elusive skill. Many aspire but few can meet the brevity, clarity, turn of phrase and perspicacity needed. In this fifth compendium, Malcolm once again demonstrates he can and does. He questions, illuminates and chides in equal measure across an impressive array of topics, from the demise of an apostrophe in Harrogate to the number of petals adorning the rose on a Yorkshire cricketer's cap. His tone is equally varied, from downright irritation through simple pleasure to rank bewilderment. Remarkably, he blends Yorkshire grit and cavalier flamboyance. Who else could ask, as captain of a side that contained Geoffrey Boycott, "does anyone open the innings?"

General Sir Jack Deverell KCB OBE DL
Commander-in Chief Allied Forces Northern Europe
2001 - 2004

Cricketer

Trust me, there's plenty to choose from the Watson canon. So let me settle on one particular note, inspired by tales from the Oval Test of 1976 and Malcolm's own memories of a calypso record that was heard around the ground called *Who's Groveling Now?* He was there that Saturday, soaking it up; and needless to say, he still has his copy of the old 45 RPM record, autographed later by Michael Holding. He signed off his note to me with an attachment containing the lyrics, with the words "as far as I can understand them..." Playful, knowing, self-deprecating: that's Malcolm. He makes you feel like it really matters, that all the details count. They don't make 'em like him anymore. More's the pity.

Phil Walker
Editor-in-chief, *Wisden Cricket Monthly*

Man of Letters

Many of Malcolm's letters to the national press and specialist magazines concern cricket. His missives to the Isle of Wight County Press, of which I was editor for 16 years, are usually on more localised matters. But as a fellow student of "The summer game" I would make the following analogy. If I were to cast Malcolm as a cricketer it would have to be Sir Curtly Ambrose. His letters are like Curtly's deliveries: short, testing and constantly 'on the money'. As a local newspaper editor, I regularly had to sort the wheat from the chaff, with many boring, repetitive and, frankly, deranged offerings landing on my desk. Malcolm's were always a breath of fresh air. May my successors receive many more!

Alan Marriott
Former editor, *Isle of Wight County Press*

CONTENTS

INTRODUCTION

This fifth volume runs from the 1 July 2020 to 30 June 2023. The format remains the same as the last three, with a section on Travel offering tips and recommendations to the *Telegraph* and the *Sunday Times* travel sections; and another, Extras, for additional submissions and correspondence. Here then are the latest published letters and other items, along with many more that weren't published, during this period.

The main recipients continue to be the *Times* and *Telegraph* newspapers. Next came the *Evening Standard*, though its letters page, already reduced to as few as two letters a day, has now dropped its letters column altogether. *Country Life* features strongly. A welcome return has been made to *The Oldie* with three letters in a row in 2020, after an absence of six years.

As to clues to content that will attract the eyes of editors of letters pages: in the case of *The Times*, in addition to succinctness and courtesy, I find that their description of "interesting is good, quirkiness is better and humour is best of all when we need to fill an awkward hole in the jigsaw" remains valid guidance; and I continue to be guided by advice that *The Daily Telegraph* letters page, as well as being about important things, also specialises in "whimsy and wry observations about daily life".

I hope you find that at least some of these latest offerings meet these criteria.

A new recipient in this volume is the *Stamp Magazine* in which four letters have been published, with one each about postage stamps in *Country Life* and *Cigar Aficionado*, following a lifetime's interest in the hobby. A second new recipient is *Wisden Cricket Monthly*, whose editor-in-chief has kindly provided one of the forewords.

Finally, as we enter our sixth year here, it seems appropriate that the Isle of Wight press features more prominently, with another foreword provided by the outgoing editor of the Isle of Wight County Press; and some words of endorsement on the back cover written by a prolific author, journalist and broadcaster finding time from his recently acquired cottage a street away.

Malcolm Watson

Ryde
Isle of Wight

July 2023

PREFACE

Published letters that follow are in a larger font to distinguish them from the others, which were unpublished and in a smaller font. Both have the subject heading in bold.

The letters, or other submissions, are shown in date order as a reminder of some of the issues of the day. The dates shown are the date of publication, or the date of submission for those not published. Dates shown as references are in the format used in each publication.

The titles *The Daily Telegraph* and *The Sunday Telegraph* have been abbreviated to *DTel* and *STel* for unpublished letters and the definite article dropped for published letters to save space. Salutations, or none, are as used in the individual publications.

All letters have been signed from Malcolm Watson, or as shown.

Rank has only been used when there is some military content, or other reason, to give credibility to the points being made.

Letters in the *Telegraph* newspapers with the picture are shown in bold, except where the picture accompanies the leading subject of the day. Letters published with a picture have (P) after the title. In all cases, the actual title of published letters is used and will be that for the group of letters when there was more than one. Entries in the *Sunday Times Culture* section have the subject in bold in the text.

Where some letters seem to be repeated at later dates, they have been included to demonstrate the determination to get the subject aired, or share the wit. When such letters were sent to different publications on roughly the same dates, they may be shown together as a single entry.

Entries in italics are from other sources, for material edited out, or for notes by way of explanation.

WHERE WE
LEFT OFF

Evening Standard   28 Nov 19

When is a vote not a vote

I was surprised to hear and read about Lord Heseltine saying *on BBC Radio 4's Today*, "I cannot vote or support people who are going to make the country poorer and less influential - full stop, end of story" ["Hezza: Vote Lib Dem or Independent", November 26]. As a member of the House of Lords he cannot vote in the general election - full stop, end of story.

The Times   11 Dec 19

Lush liebfraumilch

Sir, You report that the Britons are once again lapping up liebfraumilch ('Roll out the riesling, German wines are making a comeback' Dec 9) and that sales are soaring in upmarket establishments. I wonder if this extends to London's clubland? In Somerset Maugham's novel *Cakes and Ale*

the narrator is taken to a club in St James's
Street where his host asks the steward "for
some of the Liebraumilch, the '21", adding
that: "I want my guest to see that we know
what's what here."

Sunday Times   26 Jan 20
Sport section

(Gents v Players)

The England Test team with eight players
privately educated (last week) brought back
memories of attending the last Gentlemen v
Players match at the Scarborough Festival in
1962. Ten of the Gentlemen team were
Blues and one school, Tonbridge, provides
the number two: now Zak Crawley, then
Roger Prideaux. The Gentlemen hadn't
won the twice-yearly match since 1953,
when they won both. I would expect the
privately educated side of today would get
the better of the rest if such a festival match
could be revived. Played at the end of the

season it could also act as an entertaining pre-tour trial.

The following letter appeared in the book of unpublished letters to the Daily Telegraph, *titled* You Couldn't Make It Up...! (2020)

When your number's up

SIR - To make the most of the palindromic date of my birthday - 02/02/2020 - at 1221 I shall be enjoying a drink; at 1331, I will be having lunch; at 1441, smoking a celebratory cigar; and at 1551, watching the France v England rugby match on television. The times 2002, 2112, 2222 and 2332 will pass slowly until reading Monday's letters online from 0000 to see if I have made it.

DTel   **Hands off approach to marriage**   23 Mar 20

SIR - Those bringing their weddings forward (Letters, March 23) may not be taking their social-distancing responsibilities as seriously as they might.

2020

DTel	**Predictable predictions**	2 Jul

SIR - Judith Woods dismisses *Superforecasting* by
Philip Tetlock and Dan Gardner as "a hefty 350-pager
on how historical patterns can be used to accurately
predict the future" ("Could anything be worse than an
awayday with Dominic Cummings?", July 2). I
predict that she hasn't read the book and in doing so
that I achieve a Brier score of 0 (perfection).

The Times	**Free milk**	4 Jul

Sir, Not all of us poured our one third of a pint of
milk on to the playground grass like Matthew Parris
(Comment, July 4). In my house at boarding school
unclaimed milk was free to anyone else after 9pm. I
remember making and eating 23 consecutive
Creamola caramel custards in short order - until I
went off them.

DTel	**Persian cats**	6 Jul

SIR - I was amused to read that Tim Stanley had slept
in Los Angeles on a mattress on the floor of a Persian
car dealer ("Trump's fate in culture war is now all he
has left", July 6). Or could that have been a dealer in
Persian cats ?

Carpets?!

The Times   **Australia**   9 Jul

Sir, Will Humphries is mistaken in describing
Australia as a former colony ("Philip's swipe over
Australia's grievance", July 9).   The Commonwealth
of Australia, now a sovereign country, is a former
dominion formed of six separate former British self-
governing colonies of Queensland, New South Wales,
Victoria, Tasmania, South Australia and Western
Australia. On 1 January 1901, the colonies collectively
became states of the Commonwealth of Australia.
The Northern Territory was transferred from the
control of the South Australian government to the
federal parliament in 1911.

The Times   **Nah!**   11 Jun

Sir, Like Deborah Ross with *Ticket to Ride* and *Ticket
to Ryde*, since 1968 I have been singing the refrain of
the Beatles' *Hey Jude* as *la-la-la la* until seeing it written
down fairly recently (Times 2, July 9; letters, July 11).

   Of the five having lunch in the garden on Saturday
only one knew it was *na-na-na*.

The Spectator   **'Reverse swing'**   12 Jul

Sir: Charlie Campbell ignores a key requirement in
his novel solution to 'reverse swing' ('Cricket balls',
11 July). While tongue must remain in-cheek, using

different brands of hand sanitiser for each side of the ball will not get it reversing in no time, as one side of the ball still has to be left dry and rough for it to do so.

DTel **Dropping James Anderson** 15 Jul

SIR - Scyld Berry is right ("Time to drop Anderson and put faith in Archer", Sport, July 15). Must we really wait for James Anderson to move from 587 to 600 Test wickets? After all, in the days when only three men had achieved 300, Derek Underwood was left on 297.

Anderson went on take his 600th Test wicket on 25 Aug 2020 against Pakistan at the Ageas Bowl. He has 688 Test wickets at the time of publication.

STel **Social distances** 15 Jul

SIR - A Department of Transport official has said of social distancing that a local authority can include the imperial units (6ft 6in) on the signs if they wish (Coronavirus, Regulations, July 12). However, the social distance in UK was described in the 51-page government recovery strategy paper *Our Plan to Rebuild* (updated June 12) as "two metres (6ft)". No doubt this was not because two metres measure six feet, but because six feet are two yards, thus making two yards a sensible and equally memorable approximation of two metres.

The Times	**Jumbo comparisons**	18 Jul

Sir, You say that if Concorde was a Ferrari, the no-frills functionality of the Boeing 747 "jumbo jet" was more akin to a Ford Fiesta (Leading article, "Grounded", July 18). But as you also highlight the jumbo's generous capacity, it was surely even more akin to a Ford Granada Estate.

The Cricketer	**Dexter chose Gray-Nicholls**	19 Jul

Huw Turbervill is mistaken in saying that Slazenger was the bat of choice for Ted Dexter (August). I have searched my cricket library and schoolboy cuttings for a photograph of him carrying a Gradidge or Slazenger bat, though I did not expect to find one. However, I did come across a 1961 advertisement for Gray-Nicolls in which he says: "I have used Gray-Nicolls bats ever since I started playing 1st-class cricket and find them to be the finest on the market and a pleasure to use." I certainly never saw him bat with anything else.

Acknowledged, Malcolm. Read it somewhere. Obviously erroneous. All best wishes. (Huw Turbervill)

Country Life   22 Jul

On a sticky wicket

James Fisher says that James Anderson is the greatest fast bowler to play the game (*'It really is cricket', July* 8). Based on the highest number of Test wickets among fast bowlers - his 584 wickets at an average of 26.83 in 151 Tests *currently** - this is mistaken. Statistically, the most consistently successful Test fast bowler of all time is England's Sydney Barnes who, between 1901-14, took 189 *wickets** in only 27 Tests: a phenomenal average of 16.43. Let us not be fooled by the *large* increase in Tests *played during careers in the modern era**, enabling James Anderson to take three times as many wickets, but in five times as many Tests - magnificent though his record haul is.

*Italics omitted.

Anderson's statistics at the time of publication are 688 wickets at an average of 26.21 and aged 40.

Daily Telegraph   31 Jul
Sport section

County conferences unthinkable

The return of first-class cricket in the form
of the Bob Willis Trophy is more than
welcome, but I sincerely hope that, as Scyld
Berry wonders (July 24), the 18 counties will
not then in future play each other annually
in three conferences, home and away,
making 10 games each, plus a final. As a
Yorkshire member for 56 years and since
living in the South, I have been able to
watch them play in the County
Championship at Arundel, Canterbury,
Chelmsford, Hove, London, Southampton
and Taunton. Travelling to Leicester for
their southernmost championship match
does not bear thinking about; though a
place in the final this year does. Let's hope
by then spectators may be allowed in.

I should have included Worcester as well.

The Times **Kitchen gifts** 31 Jul

Sir, Regarding kitchen-related and jewellery presents (letters, Jul 31), after the birth of our third child I gave my wife what I called an eternity television - for use in the kitchen. The latest has been a hob with gas rings, a winner during lockdown.

The Oldie August issue

Bloody Mary's sidekicks

SIR: Bill Knott is spot on with the ingredients that make a perfect Bloody Mary, especially with the additions of celery salt and sherry (July issue), but the names he uses for the varieties need expanding on.

A Red Snapper was the original name for the cocktail devised in the King Cole Room of the St Regis Hotel in New York, where it is still vodka-based and called that name.

Elsewhere, Red Snapper has been adopted for the gin-based variant. Adding the liquor from a jar of sliced jalapeños, as he suggests, may lend a sour Mexican edge to a Bloody Mary, but Bloody Maria is the name used for the tequila-based version.

For the full vodka-based set, a Bloodshot has half tomato juice, half beef consommé; and a Bull Shot has consommé but no tomato juice.

Isle of Wight   7 Aug
County Press

Covid by car

I fear that John Heelan is mistaken (CP letters, 31-07-20) if he thinks that baby boomer second-homers on the Island will spread Covid-19 via public transport services.

They will travel by car, probably their second, or even third.

DTel   **Aging pace bowlers**   7 Aug
Sport section

Scyld Berry suggests that James Anderson is the best 38-year-old pace bowler there has ever been (*England are wasting their best hope of winning the Ashes, 6*

August). That accolade surely goes to England's
Sydney Barnes whose 49 wickets taken at the age of
40 in the 1913-14 series against South Africa is still a
series record - and he missed the fifth Test. Retiring
then with the unrivalled average of 16.43 from 189
wickets in 27 Tests, it is Barnes who is the unique
phenomenon, magnificent as Anderson's
achievements are.

Sunday Times   9 Aug
Culture section

You Say

It is hard to imagine a sign in a library in
post-British India saying "Math", *but there it
was in **A Suitable Boy** (BBC1).*

Words in italics omitted as already referenced.

DTel   **James Bond at sixes and sevens**   11 Aug

SIR - Madeline Grant and, it appears *Radio Times*
magazine, are wrong to say that only six actors have
graced the role of James Bond in films ("Bond fans
want humour and seduction, not tortured wokery",
August 11). David Niven is the seventh, starring in
Casino Royale (1967). Whatever the results of polling

of tens of thousands of the magazine's readers in a knock-out tournament between the six actors, it is worth remembering that David Niven had been Ian Fleming's choice when Sean Connery was cast as Bond in 1961, Niven reflecting the author's image of the role.

Isle of Wight   21 Aug
County Press

New app a step backwards?

In May, my wife and I successfully downloaded the NHS contact-tracing app for trial on the IW onto our iPhone 6 and iPhone 7, smart enough Apple phones for our needs.

On Friday, we were eager to download the latest NHS COVID-19 app on hearing that the Island is to be part of a new trial, but were unable to do so on the iPhone 6, as Apple phones must now be iPhone 6S and newer.

After all the concern about the paucity of phones being smart enough for the discarded app, one type that was smart enough is not any longer.

No one is going to upgrade their smart phone for an NHS app.

You couldn't make this up.

Daily Telegraph   22 Aug

Passport blues

SIR - Looking at old style passports (Letters, August 21), mine (issued in 1969) is blue - but all later versions, from 1977, are black.

I always imagined that the latter group had been phased in after joining the European Economic Community in 1973.

Sunday Times   **Bathrooms in the USA**   23 Aug

Gabrielle Fletcher has mistranslated in part the use of "bathroom" in the USA (Letters, last week). It does not include a "lonely lavatory": (usually) with a basin, that is known as a half bathroom.

The Oldie   September issue

Can Boris tie his bow tie?

SIR: Grahame Jones (Letters, August issue) is quite wrong to say that Boris Johnson is shown sporting a clip-on bow tie in the photograph taken at the Christ Church Ball, Oxford, in 1985 (The Way They Lived Then, July issue). The fastener that's showing enables the neckband to be connected in a loop and would not be seen when the collar is turned down.

A clip-on bow tie has no neckband and is pre-tied with two clips to clip under the two sides of a folded down collar.

Whether Boris Johnson's bow tie - worn with a winged collar - is pre-tied or not is another matter altogether.

See also page 202.

DTel   **Treasury refunds**   31 Aug

SIR - Molly Kingsley says that parents must be paid back their taxes for weeks of schooling missed ("We working parents have had enough", August 31). I wonder where that leaves the taxes of the much smaller group of parents who do not use state education at all - with the Treasury where they belong and with no expectation of a refund.

Evening Standard   **Woman's Hour**   7 Sep

Had there been a Man's Hour from which the lead presenters were to step down there would have been a clamour for neither the presenters to be replaced nor the programme to continue ["Barnett to host 'Radio mothership' Woman's Hour", Sept 7]. It is surprising that Woman's Hour can survive into the 2020s.
J M C Watson

The Times   **Happiness is a cigar named...**   8 Sep

Sir, To borrow from Rudyard Kipling* about a woman and a cigar: a film is only a film but a Hamlet is a good cigar (letter, Sep 8).

"A woman is only a woman but a good cigar is a smoke."

Sunday Times **You say** 9 Sep
Culture section

Drinking beer from a bottle at Siegfried's dining room
table in **All Creatures Great and Small** (C5) - I don't
think so.

DTel **PMs' children** 14 Sep

SIR - Rather than Wilfred Johnson being only the
third baby born to a serving prime minister in living
memory (News, September 14), three of the last five
prime ministers have been so blessed and in less than
a generation. A fourth, Gordon Brown, entered No 10
with a one-year-old. The present trends for older
parents and younger prime ministers would seem to
make this ever more likely.

DTel **Face masks** 16 Sep

SIR - I wonder why the Duchess of Cambridge always
seems to wear her face masks upside down
(Photograph, front page, September 16). The folds
should point downwards.

The Times **Cricket in 2020** 17 Sep

Sir, Your extract from the archive (Cricket in 1920, Sep 16) starts with: "In the whole history of cricket there can have been few more interesting seasons than that which ended yesterday at the Oval". Today, the 2020 season, with the completion of the men's international season at Old Trafford on Wednesday, is proving as interesting as any season here since, with a loss to Australia on Wednesday a reminder of what lies ahead.

The 1920 extract ends with: "The MCC team for the Test matches in Australia is a powerful combination of all the talent, and there is good hope that it will prove strong enough to win the rubber". It didn't and Australia won all five Tests, the first time this had been achieved. In 2017/18 we did not have all the talent available - Ben Stokes being absent, as he was this week - and we lost by four matches to none. Let us hope that all the talent remains fit and available for England's next attempt to regain the Ashes in Australia in 2021/22, providing a worthy extract from the archive a hundred years later.

England lost 4-0.

Wisden
Cricket Monthly

1966 and not all of that   18 Sep

Phil Walker makes the surprising assertion that the
West Indies had a long break between the Trent
Bridge and Headingley Test matches in 1966, as the
World Cup took over ("1966 and all that", October
issue). Far from being "recharged and rested", they
had played six 3-day first-class matches, five against
the counties, winning one, drawing three, losing one
against Northamptonshire and one drawn match
against the MCC President's XI at Lord's. Another 3-
day match, against Surrey, was reduced by rain to 60
overs a side, which the tourists won. What rest they
did get was restricted to several days waiting for the
rain to stop and the four Sundays which, in those
days, were rest days during matches.

I was lucky enough to be at Headingley to see
Garry Sobers hit 174 and Basil D'Oliveira hit Wes Hall
(of all people, as *Wisden* records) back over his head
for six.

Hi Malcolm

*Cheers for this, poor form on the first Test venue, sorry
about that. To see Sobers at Leeds, what a privilege. I bet
you can see it as clear as if it were yesterday.*

*Thanks again and hope you're enjoying the magazine,
venue mistakes notwithstanding.*

Phil

Phil Walker
Editor in chief | Wisden Cricket Monthly

He bet correctly.

DTel **Chance of dying** 29 Sep

SIR - You report on the front page of "a Public Health England study showing Covid patients' chances of death roughly doubled if they contracted flu at the same time" ("Elderly face winter flu vaccine shortage", September 29). I suspect it didn't say that at all, the chance of death for all patients being 100 per cent. It is the chance of dying with Covid 19 that may double if the patient also has flu.

The Oldie October issue

Three degrees of separation

SIR: What chance the subject of one letter being related to the sender of another on a different topic, who then has a third letter published in successive months?

I am Ian Carmichael's nephew (Letters, August and September issues).

See pages 16 and 21.

The Cricketer   **Military ranks**   (16 Sep)

Gulu Ezekiel has stripped M S Dhoni of his honorary
military rank in the Indian Territorial Army by three
ranks ("So flamboyant yet so cool", September).   In
2011, Dhoni was conferred the honorary rank of
lieutenant colonel, not lieutenant. He is in fact the
second Indian cricketer to receive this honour, after
Kapil Dev. In years gone by Indian touring teams
were often managed by retired and even serving
officers, so this link continues a long tradition of the
Indian military and the first-class game.
Malcolm Watson, Colonel (retd)

Was distilled down to:

The Cricketer   October issue

Dhoni's rank

Gulu Ezekiel has stripped M S Dhoni of his
honorary military rank in the Indian
Territorial Army by three notches
(September).   In 2011, Dhoni was conferred
the honorary rank of lieutenant colonel, not
lieutenant.

| *The Times* | **A roll too far** | 3 Oct |

Sir, I was interested to read about Colonel John Waddy (Obituary, Oct 3) trying to change one big scene in *A Bridge Too Far*, the one with Robert Redford capturing Nijmegen bridge, rather than a sergeant in the Grenadier Guards who was in the lead tank to cross the bridge. I was one of a group of tank crewmen stationed in West Germany who were employed as extras during the filming. Realising the importance of the scene, I managed to get myself onto the lead tank of four. We were just about to roll when we were relegated to third position as our machine gun was not one that fired; morale took a further tumble when we were told to close down the hatches. Only the lead tank commander was allowed his head out, to give a thumbs up to Robert Redford at the end of the bridge. It turned out to be a very fuzzy image.

See also page 144.

| *Sunday Times* | **You say** | 6 Oct |
| *Culture section* | | |

Why on earth did **Mastermind**, **Only Connect** and **University Challenge** follow one after the other on BBC Two? The mastermind of that scheduling needs to get connected with the audience or find a new challenge.

The Spectator **What ho!** 8 Oct

Sir: A friend of many years still greets me with "What ho! What's on?" (Letters, 10 October).

Country Life **Cigar sizes** 16 Oct

In his article about Edward Sahakian (*'The cigar revolution'*, September 23) Bolivar sees no reason why there shouldn't be a cigar size, or *vitola*, called a Sahakian in the way that we have a Churchill and a Lonsdale. Well this would be fine if the proposed cigar size (*panatela*/Corona Especial) were as widely produced as Churchills and Lonsdales are, but it is a rarity. Also, the pronunciation of the Sahakian's four syllables is unlikely to roll off the tongue, or catch on, like the other two. No, I suggest that Edward Sahakian's unique contribution to the cigar industry, brought to life and readers' attention in COUNTRY LIFE, like his opening of Davidoff of London at the corner of Jermyn Street and St James's 40 years ago, are sufficient to stand the test of time.

STel **HS2** 28 Oct

SIR - It appears that Madeleine Grant ("Tree-felling HS2 is an outrage", October 25) and Robert Readman (Letters, October 25) understand neither the purpose nor the scope of HS2. The line is being built not so that trains can run faster but because the present line has insufficient capacity to meet the demand for passenger and freight services. By transferring some intercity trains to HS2, capacity will be created on the west coast main line for additional services between London and Milton Keynes, Stafford , Stoke , Leeds , north Wales and others.

Equally important, more freight trains will be able to run, particularly to and from Felixstowe. Much of the port's freight is moved by road because of the lack of capacity on the west coast main line. The transfer of passengers and freight from road to rail will lead to the welcome result of more use of electric power and less petrol and diesel.

Any 20 to 30 minute reduction in the headline journey time between London and Birmingham will be a consequence of HS2 and never has been the reason for it.

| *The Times* | **Surname only** | 30 Oct |

Sir, I signed my first letter home from boarding school, aged eight, "Love from, Watson", to the amusement of the headmaster and my mother. I am still generally known by my surname - if I hear my wife calling me Malcolm I know I am in trouble. Fame at last (letter, Oct 30)?

Commenting on the use of surnames only for some male composers, a correspondent had ended his letter with:

"Referring to any composer (or indeed people in many other walks of life) solely by their surname is a privilege bestowed upon them as a result of their fame, not their social status."

DTel **Photo at the Oval** 4 Nov
Sport section

The picture of Jack Hobbs and Herbert Sutcliffe leaving the field at lunch on the third day of the decisive Ashes Test at the Oval in 1926 ("Pathe shows Hobbs lifting a grim year", October 24) seems strange in that the fielders and umpires have already left the field. This is borne out in the 23 minute Pathe News footage on YouTube, where the players and umpires seem to leave the field in the order of nearest to the pavilion, unless an individual hangs back to wait for someone else. It mattered not whether the interval was for rain, lunch, tea or change of innings, but could be affected by the crowd coming onto the outfield, possibly in this case. Contrast this today with the batsmen only being overtaken (and acknowledged) by their counterparts on change of innings as the openers rush to have time to put all their protective gear on in the 10 minutes allowed.

DTel **Shielding lifted** 6 Nov

SIR - Having restocked our drinks trolley for
lockdown, I see that it says on the back of the bottle of
tequila that "UK Government recommends adults do
not regularly exceed: Men 3-4 units a day Women 2-3
units a day."   Now that's what I call "not a return to
the very restrictive shielding advice", as notified in
the latest guidance for those in the clinically
extremely vulnerable category.

Sunday Times 8 Nov

War chest

If General Sir Nick Carter, chief of defence
staff (CDS), does head over to Downing
Street to confront the chancellor (News,
October 25) he won't be the first to do so.
Early in his days at Number 11, Gordon
Brown clashed with the then CDS, General
Sir Charles Guthrie, about the defence
budget. "You don't think I understand
defence, do you?" a defensive Brown said to
Guthrie. The General's reply was forthright:
"No, I bloody well don't."

The Times   **Corrections and clarifications**   19 Nov

Sir, You published a letter from me in 2015 (May 15) saying how I started to read the letters page from the bottom left, with "Corrections and clarifications", the admissions of fallibility being both welcome and informative. So far this month, there have been a surprising 17 such admissions in print in just short of 17 column inches. I now find myself turning to that section immediately after a scan of the front page, to check on fake news.

Isle of Wight   20 Nov
County Press

Filming welcome – and permitted

Robert Lilmay couldn't find any indication that making TV drama shows is an essential and protected occupation (CP, 13-11-20).

In fact this can be found in Statutory Instrument (SI) 2020 No 1200, Health Protection (No 4), where the requirement to close businesses and premises "does not prevent the use of any premises used for the making of a film, television programme, audio programme or audio-visual advertisement."

Filming of The Beast Must Die moved to our property last Friday afternoon, where "gathering" by the crew and actors was conducted under the SI exception.

The following day, the crew of 45 completed their filming at the Waterside Swimming Pool in Ryde and have left the Island, their living and working here over the last 11 weeks having been a welcome boost to the local and national economies.

We look forward to being able to see the film, which could be as early as Spring 2021.

The filming at our property did not make the final cut.

DTel   **Freezing celebration**   20 Nov

SIR - Geoff Evans asks for suggestions for a special occasion to use a box of frozen prawns (Letters, November 20). What about the arrival of a new freezer?

| *Sunday Times* | **You say** | 21 Nov |
| *Culture section* | | |

Fancy Victoria Coren Mitchell not pronouncing "protesters" correctly while hosting **HIGNFY** (BBC1).

| *The Times* | **Pink gin** | 24 Nov |

Sir, Pink gin as a cocktail is missing, surprisingly, from the good news in your guide to lockdown drinking ("Pick your poison: what that drink is doing to you", Times2, Nov 24). Measures of gin taken with dashes of Angustura bitters and water have served generations of service personnel, protecting them from seasickness and large bar bills - the cost of tonic water added to duty-free gin often being prohibitive. The bad news is the tonic and this is the best way to cut it out.

| *The Cricketer* | **Putting a hold on** | 26 Nov |
| | **back-to-back** | |

The term back-to-back (BTB) came in when *successive* Test matches were first played without the touring side having another match between them. We now seem to have BTB sixes, fours and dot balls. It appears that Nasser Hussain, the most frequent culprit, would like to take the word *successive* "out of the equation", his next most used phrase.

Presumably his most welcome articles in *The Cricketer* are made up of BTB words, consisting of BTB letters. Can you please try and help put a stop to this nonsense both on air and in print?

Thank you Malcolm; all best wishes.

The Spectator   **Film credits**   29 Nov

Sir: Fiona Mountford notes among the list of job titles in the closing credits of *The Crown* a drapes master and drapes master assistant, being the sort of roles for which many feature films can only dream ('Sets appeal', 28 November). The James Bond film *Skyfall* (2012) had both male and female draughtspersons, a male junior draughtsperson, but a female drapes master; others credited include a standby chargehand and an apprentice plasterer. With the making of film and television programmes still permitted, let us hope that as many of these gender-neutral roles as possible are out there and paying the minimum wage.

Stamp Magazine Dec/Jan issue

Whether stamps are still used for postage is really up to us

Jeff Newman is right that if you venture into a post office, it will invariably sell you a label rather than a stamp (October issue, page 32) and that's because they are financially rewarded for this policy. I discovered this when I first asked for stamps to be used instead and there was a marked reluctance to do so.

Further obstacles have also been put in my way such, as a refusal to take the stamped items over the counter during lockdown when the books I was sending to friends were deemed to be 'non-essential'. In the end they sold me the stamps which I stuck on myself and I put the packages in the postbox outside.

It is incumbent upon all of us to ask for stamps instead of labels if we wish to see them continue to be used on larger items.

My local post office now knows that I am always going to ask for stamps and accepts that their extra pocket money for printing out labels won't be coming from me.

Edited and improved. A subsequent ploy has been to say they are too busy to issue stamps.

DTel **Abandoned tour to South Africa** 7 Dec
STimes
Sport letters at both

I wonder if the ECB had a risk register for England's abandoned tour to South Africa? I suspect not; for if they had, the tour would surely not have taken place with its loss of broadcasting revenue and wasted expenditure of about £1 million, including paying for its own charter flights. Sometimes less is more - for players, teams, followers and administrators; and as the ECB chief executive has admitted on cancellation "the welfare of our players and management is paramount". The next overseas tour by England should have been the one to Australia in the winter of 2021/22.

DTel **Vaccine rollout** 8 Dec

SIR - Sarah Knapton, Science Editor, (News, December 7) poses some helpful questions about the Pfizer injections, except perhaps one: "I am 80 or over.

What happens now?" This may not of course have anything to do with Covid-19.

| The Times | **Cold and cod wars** | 12/14 Dec |

Sir, Talk of sending in the Royal Navy and echoes of the "cod wars" with Iceland in the 1970s ("Navy to board French boats", Dec 12 & letters, Dec14) reminds me of taking the captain to major promotion exam in 1976. Discussing the War Studies paper with fellow candidates, one was elated to have found two questions on the Cold War. Unfortunately for him, the second one was on the Cod War.

| *DTel* | **Sewing** | 15 Dec |

SIR - I have sown on many a button to a variety of garments in my time, but even if I didn't have a wife and three daughters I cannot for the life of me imagine why I should know how to shorten a hem ("Sorry, Woke Man, but learning to sew isn't a blow against patriarchy", December 15). Now sewing on a hatband is something I have done for all of them.

See also page 175.

Country Life   16 Dec

Up in smoke

Bolivar takes us on a tour of the Partagás
cigar factory in Havana and recalls cigars
from that famous brand (*November 25*).
Surprisingly, he didn't mention the 8-9-8, so
named after the way the cigars are
presented in a box of 25: eight in the top
row, nine in the middle, then eight. The
novel shape of the varnished box is eye-
catching and makes a handsome desk-tidy,
deep enough to hold such equally old-
fashioned items as a barrel-shaped pencil
sharpener.

The Oldie   **Batter for hot buttered rum**   23 Dec

Sir: I agree with Bill Knott (Drink, January 2021), my
favourite warming winter tipple also being hot
buttered rum; but what a rigmarole to go through
each time. Far better to have a quantity of the batter
made in advance. Here are the ingredients from
Trader Vic's Hellava Man's Cookbook:

1 pound brown sugar
¼ pound soft butter
¼ to ½ teaspoon ground nutmeg
¼ to ½ teaspoon ground cinnamon
¼ to ½ teaspoon ground cloves
Pinch of salt

Mix the sugar and butter together in a food processor until thoroughly creamed; add in the other ingredients. Put one heaped teaspoon of the batter into a cup or mug, add the rum and fill with hot water. Decorate with a cinnamon stick. Repeat as required.

DTel   **Car registration plates**   23 Dec

SIR - The registration letters AT were also assigned to Hull (Letters, December 23). When my father took delivery of a new car there in the 1950s he was asked if he had a number in mind. "No" he replied, "1066 and all that." He drove away with 1064 AT.

DTel   **Katya Adler**   27 Dec

SIR - Allison Pearson is being rather unfair in saying that the six glummest words in the English language have been "Over to Katya Adler in Brussels" (Comment, December 24). While we may now hear these words less often, the BBC's Ms Adler has always been articulate, clear, balanced and calm. She deserves a posting to a part of the world of her choice and I hope she gets one.

IoW Observer   **Whether the weather be hot...**   27 Dec

Madam, Your News feature on The Proposal (Observer, Dec 18) made interesting reading: the pub on Union Street is not "Weatherspoons" but one of Wetherspoon's; HM The Queen would not have been driving the wrong way up Union Street as she would have been driven. I have a new proposal: more checking, please!

Country Life   **Vintage 2018**   27 Dec

Thank you for helping to keep us sane during this last momentous year. I have just finished framing Annie Tempest's *Tottering-By-Gently** (*10 January 2018*) as a memento of it. I have titled it "Vintage 2018".

*Doctor: Do you adhere to the 14 units per of alcohol limit recommended for men?
Gentleman: I'm not sure, doctor. Some days 'yes', some days 'no'.

See also page 167.

DTel **Isle of Wight** 30 Dec

SIR - From Tier 1 to Tier 4 in 29 days - is this a record? So much for our help with the contact-tracing apps. I wonder what happened to them.

2021

BEER **Watney's Starlight** 4 Jan

Further to the tales of Watney's Starlight (*BEER*, summer and winter), there was a joke doing the rounds when it was introduced that it had been named as a result of a competition. One entrant had apparently suggested "Love in a Punt" - because the beer was f***ing near water.

The Times **Heseltine and democratic voices** 6 Jan

Sir, Lord Heseltine's letter to *The Times* without using his title (the first that I have seen since he was elevated to the peerage) alludes to him polishing his democratic credentials (letter, Jan 6). The key democratic voice - a vote in a general election - to remove the government, is one that as a peer he no longer has.

Over the last weeks, I understood that both he and Matthew Parris had admitted defeat over Brexit and that only Sir Max Hastings stood defiant.

I must have been wrong.

Isle of Wight   8 Jan
County Press

Fond memories of the other IW

John Young's article on Isle of Wight County in Virginia, USA, (My view, CP, 25-12-20) brought back fond memories of two visits to friends who lived there in Springfield back in 2006 and 2013.

We were taken to see St Luke's Church, the key architectural and historic feature of the district. Dating back to 1632 it is built in the gothic style, typical of rural English parish churches.

An active restoration group ensures that repairs are carried out enabling the building and grounds to be open to the public most of the year.

The cemetery is of considerable importance to Isle of Wight County's history and remains in use.

We came away with a charming Christmas tree decoration of the church which has now hung on its third tree on our own Isle of Wight, overlooking the Solent.

DTel **Covid jabs** 11 Jan

SIR - Dr Michael Fitzpatrick offers the perspective (The Surgery, January 11) that a life-threatening sudden collapse following vaccination is very rare, occurring at a rate of around one in a million doses. If offering the vaccine to 15 million people by mid-February is accepted and 15 people die from such a collapse, I wonder how many of those safely injected will opt out of the second jab and accept the lower level of protection provided by the first; never mind those still to be made the offer.

The Times 14 Jan

Chapter and verse

After being criticised for including no female authors among the books he read last year (letters, Jan 13), perhaps Michael Henderson could save face next time by featuring a work by Cecil Woodham-Smith or George Eliot.

| *DTel* | **Fast bowling pairs** | 14 Jan |
| *Sport* | | |

Simon Briggs invokes David Frith's book *The Fast Men* in support of his feature article "Celebrating 100 years of pace partnerships" (January 14). But how could he not even mention England's pairings of Larwood and Voce, and Trueman and Statham? Frith rightly covered them.

| *Isle of Wight* | 22 Jan |
| *County Press* | |

Comparisons with Singapore (P)

Glynn Brassington is mistaken in saying that the Isle of Wight is the same size as Singapore (Letters, CP, 15-01-21).

Singapore's area is nearly double the IW at 1.86 times the size.

For comparison, Anglesey is the same size as Singapore and Madeira is 1.12 times bigger.

Barbados is 1.12 and Isle of Man 1.49 times bigger than the IW.

The Times	**Cups of soup**	22 Jan

Sir, Carol Midgley asks which is the correct plural of
"Cup-a-Soups" and "Cups-a-Soup" (Times2, TV
review, Jan 22). With hyphens, Cup-a-Soups is
technically correct. But as the *a* is really *of* and there
are no hyphens in the brand, then grammatically
Cups a Soup must be the right answer too.

STel	**Close that gap**	24 Jan

SIR - I am 'clinically extremely vulnerable' (no spleen
for 50 years), but being over 70 years of age confers no
advantage in priority for the Covid-19 vaccination. In
view of the British Medical Association's convincing
argument, supported by the World Health
Organisation ("Give people second Pfizer dose
sooner, doctors urge ministers", Coronavirus, January
24), that the gap between Pfizer-BioNTech injections
could be extended to six weeks, but only in
exceptional circumstances, I would like to delay my
first dose until six weeks, not 12 weeks, in advance of
the second.   If this is permitted, my continued and
willing shielding could be to someone else's
advantage. I will ask that this be enacted when my
offer arrives.

The Times   **Delaying the first dose**   27 Jan

Sir, Clinically severely vulnerable (no spleen for 50 years) and over 70, I would willingly accept slower access to my first dose of vaccine (letters, January 27) - provided that I could be given the second dose no later than the six-week delay acceptable to the World Health Organisation "in exceptional circumstances". I am confident from what I have read that the overall effectiveness of the vaccine would thus be more beneficial for me than after a 12-week delay. I don't expect the rollout to be able to cope with such a request, but I have plenty of interests to occupy any delay and if someone who has had one dose can be assured of a second, then that would be an added bonus.

The Cricketer   **John Edrich**   28 Jan

David Frith's excellent obituary of John Edrich (February issue) ends with: "Anybody who saw him bat might today discern a passing image of his mannerisms in Rory Burns." I saw him many times and I can assure those who didn't that Rory Burns makes John Edrich look like David Gower.

Received with thanks Malcolm   1 Feb

Daily Telegraph   30 Jan

Wellies that can cope

SIR - I have a pair of perfectly serviceable green wellies bought more than 10 years ago. Attracted by the maker's reputation – "Where the rubber meets the road" – I find they are just as good across country. The maker is Dunlop, replacements cost £12.99 and they were made in Portugal.

A number of letters had been written complaining that Hunter and other luxury brands were being made in China and were of poor quality. Mine was the third under heading to try and redress the balance.

The Times   **Staycations abroad**   2 Feb

Sir, While working in Washington DC for three years we took a number of staycations along the eastern seaboard and never felt far from home (letters, Feb 1 & 2). Driving to Bar Harbor on the coast of Maine we went through Boston, Portsmouth and Bangor, coming back via Manchester and Worcester. The sign outside a bar in Portsmouth read: "New Year's Eve

Party. Every Thursday night" - we drove on to Scarborough without stopping.

See page 97 for a published version.

Evening Standard   **Conquering Covid**   4 Feb

I cannot agree with Andrew Mitchell MP and his colleagues that now is definitely not the time to cut the foreign aid budget [Londoner's Diary, February 4]. We should indeed be leading the vaccination efforts in the poor world, but by re-prioritising the reduced aid budget. It would be disappointing if this was not already being addressed in the directorate within the Foreign, Commonwealth & Development Office, revamped to ensure just such agility.

The Times   **Split infinitive**   10 Feb

Sir, Classics teacher, Hannah Sumner (letter, Feb 10), while noting that the English language is based on Latin and ancient Greek, uses a quote from Herodotus that ends with a split infinitive: "to not go unsung". Better perhaps to have used a fuller translation with no infinitive in it: "May the great and wonderful deeds - some brought forth by the Hellenes, others by barbarians - not go unsung".

The Spectator   **Mistaken impressions**   18 Feb

Sir: A correction for readers and your records, if I may (Letters, Initial impressions, 20 February)...for Lords, please read Lord's, short for Lord's (cricket) ground. From the other place we await further Lords' reform.

The Oldie   **Kitchen trials**   19 Feb

SIR: I was delighted to read that one of Gyles Brandreth's signature baked bean dishes has a poached egg on top (March issue). Two years ago, on holiday in South Africa my wife was listening to a podcast of BBC Radio 4's *Kitchen Cabinet* when she was astonished to hear my name. I had responded to their request for the best enhancement of all to baked beans on toast and had offered a poached egg (or two) on top. The panel regarded this with disdain. With such an endorsement, perhaps the panellists should get out of the kitchen more.

DTel   **The Duke of Sussex's military roles**   20 Feb

SIR - Your front page report ("Duke's sadness at giving up military roles", February 20) contends that the Duke of Sussex has been "stripped" of his military titles, but this has connotations of punishment about it. Whatever is thought of the decision and its aftermath it would have been more accurate and

fairer for those sources close to him to say that he had been "relieved" of his military duties. The statement from Buckingham Palace says that his military appointments will be returned to Her Majesty.
Colonel Malcolm Watson (ret'd)

This letter was prompted by Major General Jeremy Phipps, three weeks before he died. When it went unpublished a similar letter was sent to The Times, *the result of which can be seen at page 212. This book is published in his memory.*

The Times **Drinking from bottles** 24 Feb

Sir, I do hope that the props department of *All Creatures Great and Small* can acquire some suitable glasses for the next series (letter, Feb 24) so that the men of the 1930s vet's household do not have to continue drinking from beer bottles while sitting at the dining room table.

Sunday Times **'Bigger' stumps** 3 Mar
Sport section

Simon Hughes is being disingenuous when he says that because of the Decision Review System (DRS), cricket stumps are effectively 37 per cent larger than they were a few years ago (Last week and on Channel 4). They are of course exactly the same size for a dismissal whether bowled or lbw. The reason why

DRS went from half the ball hitting the middle of an outer stump, or the bails, for an lbw to be out, to the ball clipping a stump or the bails was because the Hawk-Eye tracking system was accurate enough to predict such clipping. Any residual inaccuracy was in effect transferred to the variation in the umpire's judgment.

The result is that if the umpire calls it right, then the bowler gets a wicket if the ball clips the wicket or bails, whether bowled or lbw. Yes, it requires better wickets than for the last two Tests, but then it provides a better balance between bat and ball; and ultimately it offers the most convincing reason why Test matches could be reduced from five to four days, without altering the likely proportion of wins, losses and drawn matches.

DTel   **Multi-year parliaments**   5 Mar

SIR - Fraser Nelson is mistaken in saying that it was the norm, in Britain, for four-year parliaments - dragged out to five years by doomed Prime Ministers (Comment, March 5). They were reduced to a maximum of five years with the Parliament Act 1911 and, apart from wartime, this remained the case until the Fixed-term Parliaments Act 2011, when the five-year term was fixed. Flexibility to reduce the term and restore the prerogative power of dissolution by repealing, or amending, the FTPA in accordance with the Conservative 2019 manifesto is still awaited.

The tried and tested system for calling elections was restored in March 2022.

The Times 8 Mar

Flavour to relish

Sir, I was surprised to see gentleman's relish listed among processed foods to which Alison Archard wishes have a 50 per cent tax applied (letter, Mar 6). To appreciate the flavour of the relish, as the instructions say on the pot, it should be used very sparingly. Even if all London's clubland, on reopening, found an increased demand for Scotch woodcock, I can't somehow imagine the tax on this spiced anchovy relish making any noticeable impact on the chancellor's overall take, members' waistlines, or the general health of the country.

DTel **Lost art of using quotations** 11 Mar

SIR - If the last few days are anything to go by, the quotation which we would most benefit from hearing right now ("We should revive the lost art of using quotations", March 11) is Clement Attlee's "A period of silence on your part would be welcome."

The Spectator   **Wrong King Edward**   12 Mar

Sir: For those who know their kings and queens, to have read "how the new HM Edward VII jumped up at dinner, crying: 'I want to pump shit' " (Letters, "What Chips heard", 13 March), conjures up an unlikely image. It was, of course, HM Edward VIII who was 'caught short'.

DTel   **Euromillions**   18 Mar

SIR - Neil Spaven's comparison between the chance of winning the Euromillions lottery being much the same as the risk of a serious adverse reaction to the AstraZenaca vaccine (Letters, March 18) may not be the one he intended. However small the chance, people buying tickets for the lottery expect to win.

DTel   **The lingo of weapons**   19 Mar

SIR - Parts of weapons stripped and assembled for cleaning in HM Forces also had their names codified in reverse (Letters, March 19). The part of the .30 inch Browning machine gun with the longest name was the screw, retaining, feed-lever, pivot-pin. As it was

the smallest part, it was better known as the grub
screw.

Sunday Times **You say** 23 Mar
Culture section

It is high time that the wardrobe department for
Death in Paradise (BBC) replaced the broken insignia
on the left shoulder of Commissioner Patterson's
uniform. Let's hope they can find one with crossed
tipstaffs for the start of the next series.

They have moved to an embroidered version.

Sunday Times **Bottom gear** 24 Mar

Jeremy Clarkson says he has a suit for funerals and
jeans for everything else, including hosting television
shows ("My life in jeans", Style, March 21). He
certainly wasn't wearing jeans in the re-run this week
of *Who Wants To Be A Millionaire?* (ITV), but
presumably his dark blue matching jacket and trouser
set wasn't a suit either, no tie being the giveaway.
Perhaps he has a life out of jeans as well.

The Times **Books for other worms** 30 Mar

Sir, Not all of us read novels for our literary
entertainment (letter, Mar 30). During lockdown, I

have tackled *The British in India* by David Gilmour, John Bolton's *The Room Where It Happened*; read *One Long and Beautiful Summer* by Duncan Hamilton and *Oblivion or Glory* by David Stafford; completed *Can I Carry Your Bags?* by Martin Johnson who died recently; and already had on the go *Beneath Another Sky* by Norman Davies and Robert Crampton's *How to Be a Beta Male*. I eagerly await the arrival of this year's *Wisden Cricketers' Almanack*.

Isle of Wight   2 Apr
County Press

Glad the 'Eye' is keeping a watch on the IW

David Cleghorn asks whether we should be pleased or disturbed that the IW gets several mentions in the current Private Eye (CP, 12-03-21) and, I might add, more since.

Private Eye is not just cartoons and satire; its investigative journalism and long memory are worth the subscription alone.

Two consecutive reports on the appeal by the Freshwater Five are more comprehensive than anything I have read elsewhere.

Incorrect names of councils, including the IW, have had a good run, being corrected along the way in the letters pages.

Personally, I'm not remotely disturbed by these mentions, but perhaps they might have an adverse view on the saga of the Cowes floating bridge to disturb others.

As they say in the magazine's Pedantry Corner, I must get out more, but I have been told to shield until 31 March.

The Times	**Vaccination clot**	7 Apr

Sir, If only the vaccination passport problem could be solved as easily as CM Humphries suggests (letter, Apr 7). I have had a Pfizer jab, but got no card or date for the second injection; my wife was given a card after her AstraZenaca version giving the date of her second. Such a difference could only result from a clot handling the roll-out of the vaccines.

Country Life   8 Apr

Old stamping grounds (P)

I too have a pair of imperforate 1841 2d
stamps, so I thought I'd see if I could match
Revd Chris Probert's collection of about 170
Japanese maples *(Letters, March 24)*. I have
107 stamps from Japan and, as he lives in
Normandy, 241 from France, both up to
1936. Colours include rose, lilac, violet, lake
and slate - and it has been a pleasure to get
reacquainted with them.

*The letter was accompanied by a picture of rose-
and lilac-coloured stamps of Japan of 1875 from
my collection.*

DTel   **Census calls**   9 Apr

SIR - A visiting census official made notes that I had
complied online and that I had also confirmed this by
telephone (Letters, April 9). He left saying that I
could get more visits as they were paid to make them.

Sir, Andrew Rootes rather misses the point by effectively restricting recognition for distinguished service, or acts, to the work environment or local community (letter, April 9). The few citations for honours that I have been involved with invariably end with "richly deserving of public recognition", or similar words. Many more are nominated in this way than receive recognition, for which those selected can be justly proud in the nation at large.

The Times   **Game of names**   20 Apr

Sir, Further to the name of Ida being mistakenly used (letter, Apr 19), the favoured and frequent exclamation of a fellow cadet in our platoon at Sandhurst was "f***ing Ada", as in aide-de-camp, which he later became. He has been Ada to us ever since.

Evening Standard   **Long may she reign**   20 Apr

I am surprised that Anne McElvoy can write with such confidence that when the Prince of Wales takes the throne, he will already be in his late seventies [Comment, April 21]; that is in six or seven years' time. There are actuarial assessments that the Queen could live to be 116.
The Queen died when he was 96 .

The Times **Tuck it in** 22 Apr

Sir, The digital re-creation of 1950s Thames riverside bathing by Julia Fullerton-Batten (News, Apr 21) contains some credible vignettes, but one that is not. The boy in the sleeveless Fair Isle pullover would not have had his shirt hanging outside his trousers.

DTel **Car rites of passage** 27 Apr

SIR - I was interested to read that Erin Baker had called her first car, a black B-reg Austin Metro, Bertha (Comment, April 27). Our eldest daughter called her first car, a white K-reg Ford Fiesta, Basil, because it was always faulty.

I would add the thought that adulthood came to our daughters not with the jangling of keys, but with the eventual move from being named drivers to taking on the insurance themselves.

Evening Standard **War of words** 27 Apr

The only thing that is clear in the war of words between the Prime Minister and Dominic Cummings [Front page, April 27] is that "recollections may vary".

| *The Times* | **Rebranding – giving it time** | 28 Apr |

Sir, I read with interest about the widespread derision of Standard Life Aberdeen being rebranded as Abrdn (leading article , Apr 27). In 2000, I witnessed a similar reaction when QinetiQ emerged from a similarly expensive rebranding exercise for the research and development establishments within the Ministry of Defence.

As part of the transformation, and for a significant fee, Clive Woodward, the England Rugby Union coach had been engaged to talk to us at an away-day in Bournemouth. I felt proud to be have been there wearing what was revealed as the same brightly coloured corduroy trousers that the England team had been given as part of their own rebranding.

England went on to win the World Cup three years later and QinetiQ is held now as a most successful offshoot in the FTSE 250.

| *The Times* | **French cricket** | 30 Apr |

Sir, The joint training exercise and dinner with the French cadets from Saint-Cyr (letter, Apr 30) were cancelled during my time at Sandhurst because of civil unrest in France during the summer of 1968.

Due to be held in France and a highlight of the year, the exercise would have involved the small number of cadets who had trained as parachutists jumping in a tactical setting.

A replacement exercise was arranged, for our cadets only, in the Stanford training area in Norfolk, but its stature was somewhat reduced as, after parachuting in, I was allowed to get into a land rover and be driven back to play cricket for the academy.

Stamp Magazine   May issue

Certainly, George V would not have been amused

Philip Stoy asks what King George V would have thought about today's gimmicky stamp issues worldwide (March issue, page 28). Well, he stated his views in advance.

In an autobiography titled *Another Part of the Wood*, the distinguished art historian and critic Kenneth Clark recorded a conversation in which the King said:

'I want you to make me a promise. Never allow them to make all those fancy issues of stamps like some ridiculous places like San Marino. We invented the postage stamp. All it had on was the sovereign's head and Postage and its value. That's all we want.'

DTel   **Inn on the Beach**   9 May

SIR - Rowan Pelling measures her favourite beaches
by the resuscitative excellence of three hostelries, a
short walk from the beaches at Aldeburgh,
Kingsdown and Blakeney (Comment, May 8). Our
favourite is the Rashleigh Inn at Polkerris in
Cornwall, which is actually on the beach and was
known when we went there as a young family as
"having something for everyone".

The Times   **Half terms**   11 May

Sir, I was surprised to read that Benenden had half
terms before 1961 (letter, May 11). Of the 31 terms I
spent at boarding school between 1956 and 1966 none
had a half term. In fact, exeats could not include a
night away. Perhaps boys' schools were different.

The Spectator   **Elvis, the body**   16 May

Sir: Taki's memory must be slipping to have included
Elvis Presley in a list of rock stars who died young
and had a good-looking corpse (High Life, 15 May).
Elvis had reportedly reached 25 stone when he died
of a heart attack in 1977 aged 42. Descriptions of his
body that led to this condition can be found online,
but are more suitable for a medical journal than here.

STel   **Avro Vulcan**   16 May

SIR - Your caption to the photograph of the Avro
Vulcan high-altitude strategic bomber (Roundel
refresh, News, May 16) describes it as tailless. While
it has no horizontal tailplane, it has a single swept tail
fin with a single rudder on the trailing edge, not
obvious when viewed from above, but essential for
stability during flight.

Evening Standard   **Inherited female titles**   20 May

Helen Nall is mistaken about the 92 hereditary peers
who continue to sit in the House of Lords being ring-
fenced for men [Letters, May 20]. Five hereditary
peeresses were elected in 1999; three have since died,
and the other two retired in 2014 and 2020. Also, a
significant number of hereditary peerage titles may
pass in the female line whose holders are also eligible
for election to the 92.

The Times   **Chorizo – one more time**   21 May

Sir, I lived in Mexico for three years and have always
mispronounced the dreaded sausage as "she-rots-so"
(letters, 19, 20 &21). But then I don't actually like it.

*There had been a protracted correspondence offering up
"cho-ree-tso", "cho-ree-tho", cho-ree-so"and "cho-ri-so" as*

the correct pronunciation in various parts of South America.

DTel **Pimm's** 31 May

SIR - I am down to my last bottle of Vodka Pimm's (No 6) and it appears that they have stopped production once again. While Pimm's No 1 (gin) is still available there are alternatives to imitations ("Pimm's loses out to Aldi discount rival", May 29). To reproduce them, including Nos 2 (Scotch whisky), 3 (brandy), 4 (rye whisky), 5 (dark rum), add to two parts of the chosen spirit, one part orange curaçao and one part red martini. Ensure you mix the resulting fruit cup with sufficient lemonade or ginger ale, which needs to be much more that the three parts suggested by Pimm's on their bottles.

Cigar Aficionado May/June issue

(Stamp collecting and cigars)

Dear Marvin,

Two days before reading the article on stamp collecting ["Good Life Guide", March/April 2021], which featured the rare Upside Down Jenny, I saw in the British national press a photograph of a block of four of this most famous stamp mistake in American history. Readers may be interested to know that it is due to be auctioned at Sotheby's New York in June and is expected to attract bids of more than $4 million*.

When I inherited my grandfather's collection in 1969, some of his accessories were kept in a cigar box. I expect this was common practice back then and even today cigar boxes are particularly useful for storing stamps still on paper, or in cellophane packages. As a third-generation stamp collector I have consolidated six collections, while at the same time created a second Great Britain collection for any of the next generation who might take an interest. Sadly, none does. My three daughters were much more interested in inspecting the bands on cigars I brought back from Cuba - 1997 to 2000 - and checking them against fakes they found on the Internet!

I well remember the resistance put up in "Out of the Humidor" when you decided to widen the scope of the magazine. What a success that has been. By including stamp collecting you have unearthed a connection between the hobby and cigars, which many may not have known existed.

It sold for £3.4 million ($4.82 million).

Sunday Times	**You say**	5 Jun
Culture section		

As if there aren't enough unexpected scenes appearing in **Anne Boleyn** (C5), up pops a stainless steel surgical instrument.

Sunday Times	**Acronyms**	6 Jun

Further to the subject of unfortunate acronyms (Letters, last two weeks), when I arrived on posting at the officers' mess in Sek Kong, Hong Kong in January 1970 during an exercise, the sign on a land rover parked outside showed it belonged to the Chief Umpire New Territories (****).

A correspondent had written that as a young solicitor he was instructed by a client to register the company name Southern Hemisphere Investment Trust, but the companies registry objected to the name on the grounds of its initials.

The Times **Maths for the future** 10 Jun

Sir, It is disconcerting to read that mathematics teaching in our schools is in crisis and about the impact of this on the next generation of mathematicians and scientists (letter, June 10). It is time to remind ourselves just how essential mathematics is. All buildings, bridges and machines, whether operating on land, in or on the sea, in the air and now in space, are all based on maths. The future is not sustainable without it, or those who understand and can apply it.

DTel **Soiled appearance** 10 Jun

SIR - Surely Dominic Sibley had enough time to get his sleeveless England pullover cleaned after the Lord's Test match before opening the batting in it covered in soil three days later at Edgbaston? Zero-tolerance seems to be the watchword for everything except turnout. What a pity.

The Oldie **Smarties** 13 Jun

SIR: I enjoyed reading Philip Norman's piece on Smarties (June issue) which brought back many memories, particularly of the boxes for 1s 6d.

However, my recollection of the flavours differs slightly. It was the light-brown ones that were coffee-flavoured; the dark-brown ones had plain-chocolate centres, as did the red ones.

Also in the 1950s, the lids were made of what seemed to be a form of metallic cap which was accessed after pealing the paper back. It fitted over rather than into the end like the plastic tops. I always assumed it contained some lead content as it was malleable, which may be why the plastic tops were introduced.

Another letter was published pointing out the difficulty of closing the tube with the metal cap and that it was probably aluminium, but not about the colours and flavours.

DTel **Money** 15 Jun

SIR - Charles Moore is being disingenuous in saying that "Everyone's money is the same" when it comes to cash (Notebook, June 15). Your correspondents continue to regale us with the difficulties they have in opening bank accounts to take money from their charities and other small enterprises. Character and circumstances of the person trying to pay it in have not always come over as "irrelevant" either.

| *The Times* | **Kipling** | 18 Jun |

Sir, He who keeps his head while all around are losing theirs…may not be fully in the picture.

| *The Times* | **Mispronunciations** | 24 Jun |

Sir, Oliver Kamm suggests some mispronunciations are genuine errors (Thunderer, June 23 and letter, June 24) and what they show is that a speaker knows a word from having read it rather than heard it. Unfortunately, this is not necessarily the case when words are both a noun and a verb, such as *dispute*, *protest* and *impact*, where the first syllable is emphasised in the noun and second in the verb. These differences need to be taught; but who is teaching the teachers if even those reading the news and in parliament get them wrong?

Isle of Wight   25 Jun
County Press

Availability differs from reliability

I read our MP Bob Seely's vision on ferries with great interest, but he mixes up reliability with availability.

It is availability that "has been above 95 percent" not reliability.

It is important to understand the difference.

Availability, also known as operational availability, is expressed as the percentage of time that a ferry is operating compared to its total scheduled operating time.

Reliability is expressed as the duration of operation without failure and will influence the number of ferries, spares and the repair policy required to meet a given availability.

It is availability that customer expectations are built upon; reliability is the concern of the operators.

DTel　　　　　　　**Et as in apple**　　　　　28 Jun

SIR - Andrew Gray can be assured that people in England still say *et* rather than *ate*, as designated in the Oxford English Dictionary (OED), but not everybody (Letters, June 28).

In 1960, at my small English prep school in East Yorkshire, our pronunciation mistress, Miss Foster, was also a stickler for *dilemma*, as in dill-emma and not die-lemma; though the second is shown as an alternative in the OED. Are there still teachers of pronunciation today whose names and lessons will be remembered in 60 years' time?

Evening Standard   **Wrong sort of school**   29 Jun

William Golding's Lord of the Flies did not have a group of very English public schoolboys stranded on an island [Letters, June 28].   Aged 6 to 12, they were too young for public school, though they were at the same boarding school - a preparatory (prep) school.

The Times   **Penalty shootouts**   29 Jun

Sir, Judging by the deception achieved in penalty shootouts, it appears that the goalies would have more success if they moved in the direction where they thought the ball was *not* going to be kicked.

The Times   **Red wine with fish**

Sir, Patrick Kidd invites us to imagine the scandal if it is discovered that Jacob Rees-Mogg, in unguarded moments, shudder, drinks red wine with fish (TMS, June 30).
    I once dined next to a friend who had recently returned after two years in France. The occasion was a black-tie dinner at which lobster was served as the main course. When it arrived, however, my friend continued to drink her red from the first course.

I enquired tentatively why she had turned down the white now being offered with the lobster. "Oh," she replied, "one never drinks the white unless one knows the grower."

The Oldie   **Ted Dexter – caught out**   30 Jun

SIR: Louise Flind recalls Ted Dexter telling her that when he captained England in Australia in 1962/63 "there were four draws and we beat them in Melbourne" (On the Road, July issue), thus joining that very small list of captains who had regained the Ashes Down Under. Possibly she misheard him. There were three draws and Australia also won one Test, so the series was drawn and Australia retained the Ashes, which they had held since 1958/59. Perhaps surprisingly, Mr Dexter never played for England when they beat Australia over a series.

Private Eye   **Balliwatticock**   17 Jul

Sir, I've had some nicknames in my time, but I'm glad I don't come from Ballywatticock, Newtownards, where the temperature of 31.2C on 17 July was the hottest on record in Northern Ireland.

Yours etc,

J M C Watson (Mr)

The Ed says: Thank you very much for your email and for taking the trouble to write.

Country Life   21 Jul

Throwing down the gauntlet (P)

I read with great interest the article about George IV's coronation of 1821 (*July 7*). I wore versions of many of the vestments, the wig and the shoes described when playing George IV in the lavish musical finale to the British Berlin Military Tattoo of 1983. A feature not mentioned was the last appearance of the King's Champion. The Champion was required to ride in full armour, escorted by the Earl Marshal and the Lord High Constable into the Coronation Banquet and await the challenge to all comers. The Garter King of Arms read out the challenge and the Champion threw down the gauntlet at the entrance to Westminster Hall, in the middle of the hall and, lastly, at the foot of the throne. Each time the gauntlet was recovered by Garter. This episode was an integral and popular part of the 12 performances given in Berlin. Handel's *Zadok The Priest* has been one of my desert-island discs ever since.

"A candidate for 'Letter of the week', if ever there was one", according to one follower; but see page 92.

The Times 22 Jul

Cricketing great

Sir, I keep at hand what I regard as one of those "best pieces he ever wrote" referred to in your obituary of John Woodcock (July 20). "Separated by the generations; joined by their genius" (Nov 3 2010), comparing Sir Donald Bradman and Sachin Tendulkar, included notable descriptions of other great batsmen. He said that the most complete batsman he had seen was probably Barry Richards, the most overpowering Vivian Richards, the most disarming Denis Compton, the most serene Frank Worrell, the most majestic Walter Hammond, the most dazzling Brian Lara and the most expansive Garfield Sobers. But none, he said, had Bradman's abiding dominance or Tendulkar's staying power. Among an equally small number of great cricket writers, many with similar staying power, he must have been the most complete.

DTel	**Vaccine passports**	28 Jul

SIR - James Hough wishes readers would stop comparing a vaccine passport to a driving licence (Letters, July 27) pointing out that he is not asked to show his driving licence when taking his car to a garage for fuel or repairs. A more relevant comparison is with hiring a car in person where the supplier may telephone DVLA and check what points the driver has on their licence. Demonstrating vaccine status with a passport should not require any such call.

The Times	**Tight-fisted Benny**	30 Jul

Sir, In Bob Hope's view, Jack Benny (letter, Jul 30) would have only parted with his Stradivarius when he failed to find an asbestos carrying case for it to match the suitcase he had bought to take his money with him.

*Isle of Wight
County Press*

Pricey pints!

I note the article "Bembridge's Wight Knuckle ride" (CP, 23-07-21) did not include the price of the new craft ale now on sale at the repurposed Pilot Boat Inn.

At £5 a pint the traditional footfall will be moving up the hill to the benefit of Ye Old Village Inn, where pints of various beers are still available at a much more reasonable price.

BEER   Autumn issue
(now incorporating What's Brewing)

What a pity that the commemorative edition of your excellent magazine (*BEER,* spring) celebrating 50 years of CAMRA wasn't the 50th rather than the 51st issue. I have kept them all. I won't be around to celebrate 100 years of CAMRA, but with four issues a year I hope to be still here for the 100th issue of *BEER* in 2033.

| *DTel* | **Olympic verbs** | 1 Aug |

SIR - Over the last few Olympics we have become used to *medal* and *podium* becoming verbs, but has *final* become the latest during these 2020 games; as in "It's so difficult to final for this final" in gymnastics?

| *DTel* | **Olympic verbs** | 4 Aug |

SIR - "The PM is going to staycation this year," said a senior government source (News, August 4). This must take the Gold for a noun becoming a verb during these latest Olympic games.

| *The Oldie* | **Secrets** | 15 Aug |

Sir: Rachel Johnson says that her definition of a secret is 'Something you tell only one other person' (August issue). In view of her once being known as Radio Rachel for her loose lips, presumably this is a refinement on telling only one person at a time.

| *DTel* | **Home cricket Tests** | 17 Aug |
| *Sport section* | | |

Martin Cooper (last week) is mistaken in calling for a return to two series of five Tests played in the summer: there has never been more than one five-Test series here a year. In 1965 two three-Test series

were introduced interspersed irregularly with five-
and even four-Test series when we staged the World
Cup. Since 2001 seven Tests (except six in 2019),
variously split, have been staged each summer as part
of a wider ICC programme, latterly linked to the
World Test Championship (WTC). The ICC future
tours programme beyond 2023 is eagerly awaited,
especially by those who believe that longer series are
more meaningful - even in their own right - than
single and dual matches contributing to a WTC.

The Times **UK interventions** 18 Aug

Sir, William Hague rightly concludes that the right
posture for western democracies is to be prepared to
intervene when our own security or common
humanity demands it and cites some effective
interventions (Comment, August 17). "In Sierra
Leone in 2000, a brilliant operation by the British
Army restored peace and democracy". This is true
but it was on the initiative of Brigadier David
Richards, the commander on the ground, that British
forces were used so decisively. He realised on arrival
in Freetown that he could do much more than the
non-combatant evacuation operation (NEO) that No
10 had ordered. No such opportunity will arise from
the NEO being conducted in Kabul. Brigadier
Richards went on to be head of the army and Chief of
the Defence Staff, 2010-2013.

| *DTel* | **Richard Wilson in court** | 18 Aug |

SIR - The actor Richard Wilson says that he came to fame late and as Victor Meldrew in the BBC sitcom *One Foot in the Grave* (Arts, August 18). For me and, I suspect, a generation of servicemen who undertook tours of duty in Northern Ireland in the Seventies, he will aways be Jeremy Parsons QC in *Crown Court*. Filling the 1.30 pm slot, his appearances for the prosecution at Fulchester Crown Court were compelling lunchtime viewing.

| *DTel* | **Autonomous cars** | 24 Aug |

SIR-I was interested to read of the competition run by the US Defense Advanced Research Projects Agency (Darpa) in 2004 to drive autonomous cars in the Mojave Desert in clear dry conditions and largely in straight lines ("Silicon Valley's driverless car dream is on track to fail", Business comment, August 23). I often wondered what happened following a Darpa demonstration of a US Army autonomous ground vehicle which I attended in Denver, Colorado in 1987. The vehicle kept leaving the test track and the demonstration had to be halted when it was realised that the vehicle's sensors could no longer identify the grass verge after heavy overnight snow. It is no surprise to read that for the need to avoid driving into people the dream of the driverless car is all but dead.

DTel **Social care** 7 Sep

SIR - Many MPs responding yesterday to the Prime Minister's statement on proposals for the funding of social care didn't seem to listen to the answers before asking their own pre-prepared questions. I soon found myself able predict most of the PM's answers in the House of Commons - almost word perfect - including hesitations and pauses.

DTel **County Championship** 10 Sep
Sport **or Indian Premier League**

SIR - With the fifth England-India Test match cancelled, can we hope that England's players can re-join their counties for the last three rounds of the County Championship and the match for the Bob Willis Trophy between the top two teams at Lord's starting on September 28? After such an anti-climax to the Test series, this would bring added interest to the competition with all matches already being streamed live on the internet. Or will those involved be off to the United Arab Emirates for the resumption of the Indian Premier League on September 19. (Sport, September 10)? I'm not holding my breath.

Some did return, including Chris Woakes who helped Warwickshire win the County Championship.

DTel   **Liz Truss**   16 Sep

SIR - You report that one MP describes Liz Truss as "a loner" and others call her "odd" ("Another first for Truss as she arrives at the top table", News, September 16). That fits in well with the late Enoch Powell's categorisation of women MPs as "not clubbable".

The Times   **Newtons**   20 Sep

Sir, The letters about newtons (Sep 18 & 20) reminded me of having to learn the new, to us, International System of Units (SI units) at the start of my engineering degree 50 years ago. A student who had spent a highly social first term, on opening a progress test paper at the end of it, leant across to his neighbour and whispered: "Psst. What's a bar?" Answer: "Shhh, ten to the fifth newtons per metre squared." "Newtons! What's a newton?" He left the course early.

The Times   **Chinamen and googlies**   27 Sep

Sir, Left arm unorthodox may refer to a bowler's action but not to the deliveries, which are still chinamen and googlies (letter, Sep 27). The equivalent right arm unorthodox bowler, or leg-spinner, bowls leg-breaks and googlies when bowling to a player who is right-handed. No less a cricket person than Mike Brearley, writing about the Spirit of Cricket (Sport, Mar 26, 2016), eschewed the term batter when referring to "Sarah Taylor, the England batsman". That's good enough for me, assuming that the term is not now compulsory.

Isle of Wight   2 Oct
County Press

French weapons fallacy

D. Painter is mistaken in his comments about the French (CP, 24-09-21).

First, they did not sell Exocet missiles to Argentina during the Falklands War but prior to it and before it seemed likely the two countries would enter into combat with each other.

When the war began, France embargoed weapons sales and support for Argentina.

They also allowed the British to use French ports in West Africa and provided them with information on the weapons and planes that they had sold to Argentina.

Secondly, Australia does not have a nuclear industry to have reservations about sharing any nuclear technology with France, which does.

The USA and UK will therefore be sharing nuclear propulsion technology with Australia.

There may be reasons to gloat a little over France's recent discomfiture, but let's be fair to our neighbour over the Channel in matters of fact.

The Spectator   **Ryder Cup duffers**   2 Oct

Sir: One spinoff of the monumental thrashing of Europe in the Ryder Cup (Spectator Sport, 2 October) was the sight of our top class professionals duffing their shots just like some of us ordinary golfers. For goodness' sake, there weren't even any trees on the course.

Evening Standard   **Sandhurst**   5 Oct

Officer cadets do not actually graduate, as such, from Sandhurst; they are commissioned, or pass out of the Royal Military Academy [Upfront, 5 October]. Most cadets these days have already graduated with degrees from a wide variety of universities.
J M C Watson , Commissioned August 1968

DTel **No time to leave** 7 Oct

SIR - Kevin Paton recommends remaining seated
until the very end of the credits following the new
James Bond film, *No Time to Die* (Letters, October 7).
His top secret reason for doing so could be to see the
full 163 minutes expected. I was surprised to find
that the moving pictures lasted nearer to 150
minutes.

The Times **Criminal barristers** 19 Oct

Sir, James Keely makes some interesting points in
these difficult times (letter, Oct 19), but to declare that
criminal barristers deliver first-class advocacy for the
most vulnerable people in society might be
questioned. My jury service may be statistically
insignificant, but grossed up I suspect that such
advocacy is not always on display. As with many
other challenging professions, working "punishing
hours" does not necessarily lead to success. Some of
those not remaining at the Bar may have discovered
that the calling is not for them.

Daily Telegraph   20 Oct

Cash is queen

SIR - I turn notes the right way round before putting them into my wallet so they are presented with the Queen facing the person who is being paid. I use the same discipline with foreign notes.

The second letter under the heading. Six more were published, some slightly repetitive, in bold type and with a picture on 24 Oct.

Daily Telegraph   3 Nov

How to reply to a stranger's 'See you later'

SIR - If Mr Chalwin can't resist replying, but wants to avoid verbal abuse, I suggest the equally ubiquitous: "No worries".

Other responses included: "Not if I see you first"; depending on the sex and general attractiveness of the speaker: "In your dreams";

"Your place or mine?", which had lacked any interesting follow-ups so far; and, subconsciously: "After 'while crocodile".

DT   **Yorkshire CCC**   8 Nov
Sport section

In his claim to be the first non-Yorkshire-born player to play for the county (Sport, November 5), Michael Vaughan seems to have forgotten that Lord Hawke was born in Lincolnshire. Making his debut in 1881, he went on to captain the county from 1883-1910 and was President from 1898-1938. Back then a cricketer could qualify for a county by birth or residence. Ironically it was Lord Hawke who fervently espoused the cause that only Yorkshire-born should play for the county. As the county grapples with the scandal that is engulfing it, it would do well to remember that even in Yorkshire the graveyards are full of indispensable men.

Country Life   17 Nov

Letter of the week

Bring back the cane (P)

I was interested to read the article 'Stick to it man' (GENTLEMAN'S LIFE, *November 3*), invoking the return of the gentleman's cane. A few years ago, I created one with a miniature cricket ball on top, ready for just such a revival. Ironically, I slipped and broke my ankle at Lord's Cricket Ground during the Test match in August and I am currently getting around using a traditional walking stick, that 'fine and elegant accessory' pronounced by Hardy Amies as suitable for the purpose. I am also using Nordic walking poles when venturing out a bit farther. When the time comes to do away with weight-bearing devices, I shall be there with my cricket-ball-topped walking cane to help relaunch this overdue adornment to today's gentleman's wardrobe.

The writer of the letter of the week will win a bottle of Pol Roger Brut Réserve Champagne

(P) Photo of the top of the walking stick crossed with the cane taken by me and sent in with the letter.

The Times	**Expo 2020**	29 Nov

Sir, I visited Expo '70 in Osaka, Japan where the British pavilion was also not among the best on view ("UK Expo effort is gibberish to some", & letter, Nov 29). At the 1970 fair, I saw the first-ever IMAX film and demonstrations of early mobile phones, local area networking, magnetic levitation (maglev) train technology and electric cars, all now familiar to today's travellers. From its theme of innovation and technology, I am wondering what is being shown there now that will become reality in 2070. I am sure, though, that our pavilion will still be offering fish and chips from a café.

Lord Rose, the former M&S chief, had lambasted the British pavilion at the fair in Dubai. A letter praising it was published the following day.

Expo 2020 ran from 1 October 2021 to 31 March 2022.

Cigar Aficionado   Nov/Dec issue

(Punch Cutters)

Dear Marvin,

I was most interested to read the article on punch cutters [Good Life Guide, "Punch Cutters"] in your September/October issue. I have such a cutter, which has all the merits of the ones described, but it has never occurred to me to attach it to my car keys. Instead, my .44 Magnum steel and brass bullet cigar cutter hangs from a gold and silver chain attached to my gold pocket watch. Since buying the cutter at the San Andrés factory in Veracruz, Mexico, over 20 years ago, the number of opportunities and locations to be able smoke cigars has been greatly reduced this side of the Atlantic. Consequently, I have it ready for occasions like weddings when I wear the watch and chain and a marquee has been set up with access to the open air outside.

   I have in my humidor two Montecristo 'A's and one Hoyo de Monterrey Double Corona of the same vintage awaiting such occasions when I know the razor-sharp, eight millimetre diameter circular blade will produce a punch cut ideal for savouring those long and lingering moments to remember.

Wisden Cricket Monthly   Dec issue

Hawke's 13

James Butter, a fellow lifelong Yorkshire supporter, contends that the white rose adapted by Lord Hawke as the emblem to be worn by capped players is made of 11 white petals. In fact, there are 13 petals, as a quick count on the emblem pictured in the article will indicate.

DTel   **Vaughan the batsman**   6 Dec

SIR - How reassuring to see Michael Vaughan referring to the England captain, Joe Root, as a "batsman" (*Sport*, December 4, & Letters, December 6). No doubt he will have to use the dreaded "batter" on commentary, if we are allowed to hear him.

Vaughan had been dropped from being broadcast commentating on the Test series in Australia in view of alleged comments he denied making in the racism scandal at Yorkshire CCC.

| *DTel* | **Festive films** | 20 Dec |

SIR - How dispiriting to imagine the film *White Christmas* to be boring and overrated (Letters, December 20). Whatever next - *Easter Parade*?

| *DTel* | **David Lloyd and Sky** | 22 Dec |
| *Sport section* | | |

As David Lloyd was known to say when a player was about to be dropped: "I don't know what we'd do without you - but we're about to find out."

David Lloyd had just announced his retirement from the Sky cricket commentary team.

No letters were published in the Sport section that Friday.

Return to sender

Sir, To get that Christmas card to Newmarket, New Hampshire (letter, Dec 24), Paul Grover could remove the space between N and H. The abbreviation for New Hampshire is NH. Given electronic scanning, it might just do the trick. Incidentally, I see that it is near Portsmouth, NH. I have never forgotten driving past a sign there saying: "New Year's Eve party. Every Thursday night."

2022

Stamp Magazine   Jan issue

Not the uniform of a Field Marshal

If Southern Rhodesia's definitive series of 1931-37 is known among the philatelic community as the 'Field Marshals' then they shouldn't be.

The claim that the stamp design gave King George V a change of uniform from Admiral to Field Marshal (November issue, page 47) bears closer examination.

The portrait on the stamp shows the King wearing a crossbelt over his left shoulder, which is not worn with a field marshal's uniform.

The image is almost certainly taken from the photograph in which the King is wearing the uniform of the Colonel-in-Chief of the Royal Horse Guards (The Blues).

Incidentally, there is no Order of St George, though St George does form part of the regalia of the Order of the Garter, whose badge the King is wearing in the portrait.
Malcolm Watson, Colonel (retired), Ryde

DTel	**Vaughan and England**	5 Jan
Sport section	**cricketer records**	

I cannot agree with Michael Vaughan when he says that "You live your career as an England cricketer on your Ashes record" (Sport, January 3). Neither Ted Dexter nor Mike Atherton took part in winning series against Australia. Their significant contributions as Test players have not diminished over the years and are unlikely to. Vaughan is right though that "There is probably too much focus on one series", but not "that it is what the fans remember" – at least for those whose memories stretch back into the last century.

DTel	**Worries indeed**	6 Jan

SIR – Judith Woods's instinct is right that professional settings where one's health, wealth or liberty are at stake are not suited to the use of "no worries" (Comment, "Only the woke could object to saying a weary 'no worries'", January 6). The problem is getting that accepted.

When my late father was in hospital, I asked a member of staff on the ward to stop using "no worries", during a conversation about him, as, while she may not have had any, I did. Her immediate response was: "No worries."

But see Yet More Wit and Wisdom… *page 136 for a published version.*

DTel   **Free milk**   27 Jan

SIR – At my boarding school in the early 60s left-over bottles of one third of a pint of milk could be taken after 9.00pm by whoever got to the crates first (Letters, January 27). One year I developed a liking for Creamola caramel custard, the brand with the man's face over a full moon on the packet. Each day I got enough to make a pint's worth to eat. I continued this for 23 consecutive days, after which I went off them.

Country Life   **Winners of 50 years ago**   29 Jan

I recognised immediately Juliet Mcleod's style of the horse's head in Mick Channon's favourite painting (Pneumatic, *January 26*), as I have prints of hers of two great winners of the 1970s: Brigadier Gerard and Mill Reef, who triumphed in the 2000 Guineas and the Derby respectively in 1971. The difference is that the backgrounds for those stars were expansive landscapes and not a stark stable, reflecting no doubt the amount of money available for the commissions.

I had a wager with a friend that Mill Reef would avenge his defeat by Brigadier Gerard in the 2000 Guineas next time they met. They never did and it is 50 years this year since we watched Brigadier Gerard suffer his only defeat in 18 races when beaten by Roberto, that year's Derby winner, at York. Instead, those famous winners have faced each other on the same wall at home, whether here or abroad.

STel   **Railway stations**   31 Jan

SIR – I can think of many reasons to rejoice if Michael Gove's plans to regenerate railways stations in 20 towns and cities are fully realised (News, January 30). I sincerely hope that one will be that the current trend of referring to them as "train stations" is firmly shunted into a siding and kept there.

The Times   **Backward glances**   16 Feb

Sir, Max Hastings says that the great thing in life is to move on, without backward glances (Notebook, Feb 25) – though it would appear not in the case of Brexit.

DTel   **Generation gap**   20 Feb

SIR – Sally Jones is mistaken in saying that just a generation has passed since the stubborn heroics of Dunkirk and the Blitz ("Nobody trusts us to judge the risks of a storm ourselves", February 19). Three generations have passed and we are well into the fourth since 1940/41.

It is the grandchildren and now great-grandchildren of the wartime generation that have seen stoicism morph into risk aversion, due mainly to health and safety concerns, the likelihood of litigation and unacceptable insurance costs. She is right that we can never return to that era, though it may not have been as carefree as she imagines.

Any decisions she and her parents made about skating on what she remembers as vast open stretches of ice will have been restricted to whether they might hurt themselves if they fell over. Those responsible would have taken regular readings to ensure that the thickness of the ice was sufficient for skating on it, just as would happen today.

Another letter was published on this article.

Island Life   **Cuba and Mexico**   21 Feb

Dear Ms McCarrick,

I read with particular interest the article about Cuba by Terry Willey in the February/March 2022 edition of Island Life having visited there many times myself from Mexico City. He says that he went to Guadalajara, 35 miles to the east of Holguin. However, Guadalajara is in Mexico, 350 miles west of Mexico City. Looking at a map of Cuba, I believe the place he must have gone to is Guardalavaca.

I recommend a trip to the western side of the island to the area of Pinar del Rio, where tobacco is grown, for his next visit. If I am not mistaken, it is featured in the main photograph for the article.

Yours sincerely,

Malcolm Watson
Colonel (retired)
British Defence Attaché, Havana (non-resident)
1997-2000

The author acknowledged a typing error in his dictated translation.

The Times **Palindrome and ambigram** 22 Feb

Sir, As we are invariably required to fill in dates using digital digits, 22022022 can also be read upside down making it an ambigram (letter, Feb 22). Any advance on 05022050?

Someone else got in first.

DTel **Newsnight in the future** 25 Feb

SIR – I was pleased to read that *Newsnight* will go on after the departure of Emily Maitlis and Emma Barnett (News Bulletin, Feb 25); even better if it were 'going forward', as they say.

| *The Times* | **Posthumous awards** | 7 Mar |

Sir, Your obituary of Brigadier Geoffrey Curtis (March 7) is mistaken in saying of his award of the Military Cross in 1943 that "Like all Military Cross awards, his could easily have been posthumous." Until 1997, only the Victoria Cross, George Cross and a mention in dispatches (MiD), the highest and lowest levels of gallantry decorations, could be awarded posthumously. Created on 28 December 1914, the first awards of the Military Cross did, though, include seven posthumous awards, with the word 'deceased' after the name of the recipient, from recommendations that had been raised before the recipients died of wounds or lost their lives from other causes.

| *DTel* | **Name changes** | 7 Mar |

SIR – How I so agree with Christopher Howse's distaste for the renaming of Kiev to Kyiv ("If we play chicken with Kiev the Leghorns get it next", March 5) in English usage. On the other hand, should the Prime Minister sanction a reversion from Boris to Alexander, or Al, as his family call him, that might at least provide some shock and awe.

Sunday Times
Culture section **You say** 14 Mar

Marcus Waring's Tales From A Kitchen Garden (BBC2) is a cross between **Clarkson's Farm** (Amazon Prime Video) and **James Martin's Islands To Highlands** (ITV) and has diddly squat on either of them. The script is embarrassing.

The Oldie **Bicycling at Sandhurst** 15 Mar

Sir: Mike Starke is mistaken in thinking that bicycle pedal power was revived at the Royal Military Academy, Sandhurst, in 1974 (Letters, April issue), if it had indeed ceased. In September 1966, we underwent bicycle drill in our first few weeks. The bicycles provided an efficient way of getting around the grounds to see and learn the locations and history of particular points of interest, for example the Chinese Mortar and the statue of the Prince Imperial, on which we later tested. We moved by platoon, in file and two abreast. The special drill movement I treasure was cycling to attention – sitting up with arms straight – awaiting the order "Eyes right" or "Eyes left" when passing an officer and then cycling "At ease" again. Such things we took in our stride.

On commissioning, some of us went to the Royal Armoured Corps Gunnery School, Lulworth, in Dorset, where as part of our courses to command tanks and armoured cars we were given a lesson on the "Care and use of binoculars". Sitting down on our chairs with pairs of binoculars in cases at our feet, we were told in no uncertain terms by our latest staff instructors: "Don't touch them, Gentlemen, there's a special way".

Private Eye	**Lookalikes**	21 Mar

Sir, There is an uncanny resemblance between President Zelensky of Ukraine and England's fast bowler, Mark Wood, who is off games again. Oh that he had the President's resilience.

The Times	**Endearments**	23 Mar

Sir, I am the other side of 70 from Peter Sergeant (letter, Mar 23). As far as greetings from retail assistants are concerned, he still has "My Lovely" to look forward to.

About preferred pronouns he had decided to put "Bud/Mate/Darling/Sweetie/Luvvie" after his name. Someone beat me to it with "Young man".

DTel　　　　　**Chancellor's coinage**　　　　24 Mar

SIR – Janet Daley is mistaken in attributing the phrase "sharing the proceeds of growth" to Gordon Brown's song book ("Gordon Brown 2.0 has created a new low-wage poverty trap", Comment, March 24). It was coined by David Cameron and George Osborne as leader of the opposition and shadow chancellor of the Exchequer, respectively. Until the financial crash in 2008, it was used by Mr Osborne with a frequency matched only by Theresa May's more recent "strong and stable government".

Almost a repeat of a letter published from me in the Sunday Telegraph *on 3 March 2019. See* Much More Wit and Wisdom…, *page 181.*

The Times　　　　　　　　　　　2 Apr

King of spin

Sir, Mike Atherton is right in describing Shane Warne as "the greatest leg spinner that ever lived", but I am not so sure about him being "the greatest spinner to have played the game" (sport, Mar 30), certainly when comparing Warne's 2,793 wickets in all modern formats with Wilfred Rhodes's

4,204 first-class wickets, a world record. This does not detract from Warne's unquestionable impact on the game: his revival of leg spin bowling could well mean we see his like again, though never again a haul of wickets like Rhodes's.

The Spectator	**A name dropped**	2 Apr

Sir: I find it hard to imagine that John Aspinall, who died more than 20 years ago, had, in Taki's mind, "expertise in nature and animal life matched by no one" (High life, 2 April). He calls upon a list of names longer than most for use in his column, but that of Sir David Attenborough seems to have dropped off it.

DTel	**Crisp**	4 Apr

SIR – The time has come for a Campaign for the Reintroduction of Salted and Plain (Crisp) (Letters, April 4).

A correspondent had asked why the crisps inside a packet so rarely tasted like the description on the outside of the packet.

DTel   **Post towns**   5 Apr

SIR – Jenny Farr and her daughter (Letters, April 5) should be aware that the "post town" – in their case, Hereford – is a required part of all postal addresses in the UK and Ireland, its inclusion, together with the post code, increasing the chances of the letter or parcel being delivered on time.

The only time to exclude a post town is when sending a letter for publication and the correspondent wants the village, or hamlet, to feature. That is why Ewyas Harold appeared after her name ("First-class failures") and not the city of Hereford, which she clearly had no intention of including.

Malcolm Watson
(Formerly of Welford, Berkshire)

Country Life   6 Apr

Excuse you (P)

I was most amused to see, in Tottering-by-Gently, a bowl with 'PETOMAINE'S [C]ARROTS' on it (*March 30*). Le Pétomane was the stage name of Joseph Pugol, the famous French flatulist and entertainer. Getting familiar with modern technology, perhaps Lady Tottering had seen the short humorous film *Le Pétomane* (1979) on YouTube on her laptop (*Tottering-by-Gently, March 23*), starring Leonard Rossiter in the title role, before naming the animal in question.

The Times	**Coarse putters**	22 Apr

Sir, The cover of *The Art of Coarse Golf* (1967) by Michael Green, shows a player on his knees using a club like a billiard cue, the *Walter Lindrum* stroke, named after the great snooker player (letters, Apr 21 & 22). Used most frequently to get out from underneath bushes, "many players using it have got out of trouble in as few as four shots." It is not recommended for use on the putting green "unless you are out of sight of the clubhouse, as stuffy club officials seem to object to players crawling all over the greens."

DTel	**Eating and judging food**	25 Apr

SIR - Alexandra Elletson asks why *MasterChef* judges stand up to eat (Letters, April 25). Maybe this is linked to a kitchen island being on the set rather than a kitchen table, which Jane Shilling indicates could be due to come back in vogue ("At long last my unfashionable kitchen is back in style", April 25). A new set with a kitchen table and chairs would enable those judges to eat while sitting down.

What irks me though is why so many judges insist on describing food they have tasted as *beautiful*: surely it is *delicious,* particularly on television, where we can see what they are eating?

DTel   **Banning plastic pint cups**   29 Apr

SIR - While I fully support the thrust of the letter calling for a ban on plastic pint cups ("Plastic-free pints", April 29), I defy any of the 19 well- or lesser-known signatories to confirm back where they live that "Britons are routinely charged £7 for a pint of beer". Beer around the country is still generally sold for under £5 a pint, sometimes well under. They also say that "the cups can often ruin the taste" - sometimes, perhaps. Such exaggeration is unbecoming of the lobbyists.

The Times   **Lady's drink tax**   3 May

Sir, Roger Bawden's "one pint and two halves" ploy does not solve today's problem of the "lady's drink tax" on half pints (Notebook, Apr 30 and letter, May 2). To deal with that you need to ask for "two pints and a half pint glass please". The second pint is then poured into the empty glass and drunk in two halves. "Tax" avoided.

The Times   **Resigning matters**   10 May

Sir, If Sir Keir Starmer is handed a fine by Durham police for breaking coronavirus rules he will step down as the leader of the Labour Party (Front page, May 10), demanding that Boris Johnson does likewise. In that case, Johnson could also resign as leader of the Conservatives, while remaining prime minister, as did John Major in 1995. Following Major's example, both should stand for re-election. If Johnson loses (Major won comfortably), he will resign as prime minister and the winner will be invited to form a government. The winner of the Labour Party contest will become the leader of the opposition.

The Oldie   **Commenting online**   11 May

SIR: Stephen Glover says he doesn't know of any columnists who read posts about pieces they have written, quoting the *Telegraph*, Mail Online and the Guardian Online (Media Matters, May issue). May I point out that the same is not the case at *The Times*. Mike Atherton, their chief cricket correspondent, keeps track of posts when both at home and abroad, sometimes commenting on them and acknowledging occasional errors. Jane MacQuitty, their wine critic, engages with posters about her recommendations and sometimes their scarcity; and Rose Wild enters the discussion online as would be fitting for her Feedback column.

I am sure that most people do not subscribe to a digital newspaper to comment on it, but for its content. The ability to comment is a bonus and can be fruitful, at least in these three cases.

Isle of Wight   13 May
County Press

Blair's Labour Party was best they'd ever done

In his letter chastising the prime minister 'Voters will decide Johnson's fate', (CP, 29-04-22), Steve Longford says: "the electorate will have their say at the next general election, and it is worth perhaps remembering that things didn't go terribly well for the Labour Party after Tony Blair misled parliament and the nation over weapons on (sic) mass destruction, leading to the Iraq War" in 2003.

In fact, in May 2005, Blair went on to win a third election in a row, the most won by the Labour Party in succession in 100 years of trying as the main opposition party to the Conservatives.

In other words, as well as the Labour Party has ever done.

As they say: be careful what you wish for.

DTel   **Epistolary alcohol**   26 May

SIR - William Sitwell is so right ("There's nothing wrong with drinking at work", May 26). How else could I have got over 60 letters published in the *Telegraph* in the last decade or so had I been deprived of a glass - never mind those letters unpublished? Pass the Port.
Malcolm Watson
Porto, Portugal

The Times   **Non-skiing**   28 May

Sir, Carol Midgely proudly declares that she has never been skiing and guarantees that she never will (Notebook, May 28). However, it is possible to enjoy what resorts have to offer without actually partaking in the winter sports themselves. Many years ago I went non-skiing in Alpbach in Austria. So successful was it that I later went on non-Cresta and non-bobsleigh visits to St Moritz in successive years. One of a number of advantages of these adventures was the use of a hot-bunk system whereby, coming back after nights of revelry, you slept in the bed of someone who had just left for their downhill activities. No special clothing is required save suitable boots to get around in and a warm hat.

DTel	**1950s food**	2 Jun

SIR -Dripping on toast (Letters, June 2). Luxury. At my boarding school in Yorkshire in the 1950s it was dripping sandwiches at bedtime.

The Times	**Ranking of photographs**	4 Jun

Sir, Having yet another photograph of the Duke and Duchess of Sussex on the front page (June 4) will seem inconsistent to many with describing them as "second-rank" three pages later. Images of them are surely now more suitable for occasional appearances in Olav Bjortomt's quizzes.

DTel	**The Quiet Pint**	6 Jun

SIR - Ann Sugden (Letters, June 6) may like to know that I have previously mentioned the *Telegraph* publication *The Quiet Pint,* a guide to pubs with no piped music, not only by letter* (11 June 2019), but by contacting the publications department as well. My suggestion that an updated version (last published in 2004) would once again become an indispensable companion came to naught. What a great service you would do us all by producing one this time.

See Much More Wit and Wisdom… *page 201.*

The Times	**Men in grey suits**	7 Jun

Sir, Bill Jones says that in the old days Conservative leaders were sanctioned by "unseen grey bearded grandees" (letter, Jun 7). There are plenty of contemporary accounts and photographs in Sir Alec Douglas-Home's case of the sanctioning being done by "men in grey suits" but with not a beard in sight.

DTel	**Fastest hundreds**	15 Jun

SIR - Johnny Bairstow's 77-ball hundred was the fastest for England since Gilbert Jessop's 76-ball century 120 years ago, Bairstow falling just two balls short of breaking his record (Sport, *Second LV= Insurance Test*, June 15). Interestingly, Jessop scored off 41 balls to reach his century, while Bairstow managed it with 39.

A similar letter to The Times *and* Times Diary *produced the comment from Patrick Kidd of the diary that "in Jessop's day you had to hit the ball out of the ground to get a six. He struck four more boundaries than Bairstow and I think it's fair to expect that some would have gone for six*

under modern rules, meaning he'd have reached his
hundred even earlier. Also, because of faster over rates
Jessop needed 75 minutes for his century while Bairstow
took two hours." Sent also to the Daily Telegraph Sport
section, no sport letters were published that week.

The Times	**New socks**	18 Jun

Sir, If, as Stephen Fry has suggested, it is one of life's
great pleasures to put on a new pair of socks (Robert
Crampton, Beta male, Jun 18) then, as I get older, I
find that an even greater pleasure is to discover that
they can be pulled on unassisted.

DTel	**Complaints –**	24 Jun
	to whom it may concern	

SIR - I suggest that the best way to address a
complaint to the head of a large organisation
nowadays (Letter, June 24) is to use their name and
appropriate title as these can now be invariably found
on the internet, or by checking directly with their
head office. The letter should then be signed "Yours
sincerely" and not "Yours faithfully". Putting
"Personal for" on the envelope may help as well.

The Times **Perforations** 29 Jun

Sir, Giles Coren is optimistic if he thinks that perforations in the chocolate covering of a Magnum ice cream will provide Unilever with a solution to ensure that only the area of chocolate you bite into will come away with the gooey inside (Notebook, Jun 28). The challenge has yet to be perfected for lavatory paper, which rarely tears along the perforations.

Daily Telegraph 1 Jul

When thirst collides with the price of a pint (P)

SIR - Beer was on offer at the Test match at Headingley for £6.10 a pint (Letters, June 29). I declined it.

A correspondent had been charged £6 for a pint of bitter at a pub in Norfolk and asked whether it was a record. Others reported being charged £6.60 in Tremadog in Wales, £7.20 in St David's and £1,49 for a pint of Ruddles Best Bitter in Hull (standard in a Wetherspoon's pub using a 50p voucher available to Camra members).

The Times **Defiant prime minister** 7 Jul

Sir, I much look forward to seeing Boris Johnson's final act of defiance: his resignation honours list.

Daily Telegraph **Chinaman is NOT a googly** 9 Jul
Sport section

Stephen Fry, the President Designate of MCC, is mistaken in saying that the left-arm bowler's wrong 'un [or googly] was known as a Chinaman (Interview, July 7). The left-armer bowls Chinamen *and* googlies, the Chinaman being the wrist-spun off spinner to a right-handed 'batter', their wrong 'un will turn the other way. Although it may have declined in use, the joint term remains a valid and unambiguous description of the left-arm wrist-spinner's delivery.

Sunday Times **You say** 10 Jul
Culture section

On **Just A Minute** (BBC Radio 4), Sue Perkins repeats herself with "well listened" so many times after a correct challenge for repetition that I find myself expecting a change of host for each subsequent uttering.

Deputy leaders of 11 Jul
the Conservative Party

SIR – Janet Daley is mistaken in her description of what happened when Boris Johnson was seriously ill in hospital while prime minister ("A lame duck PM is a gift to Putin, July 10). Dominic Raab took over as head of government because he was the deputy prime minister, not because he was deputy leader of the party, which he never has been. In fact there has not been a deputy leader of the Conservative Party since 2005. Before that, only four people have held the post: Reginald Maudling (1965-72), William Whitelaw (1975-91), Peter Lilley (1998-99) and Michael Ancram (2001-05).

IOW 15 Jul
Observer

Cricket correction (P)

Dear Editor,

May I be permitted to correct an error that has crept into your report of the Isle of Wight team's defeat of the Marylebone

Cricket Club (MCC) in a match at Shanklin (Sport, July 8). Thomas Lord was never the owner of MCC, but of the famous cricket ground in St John's Wood in London, hence the name Lord's (not Lords) Ground.

The Times   19 Jul

On solid ground

Sir, You report ("Easy? Old Course is unconquerable, says DeChambeau", Sport, Jul 18) that "long-time golf observers struggled to recall the ground ever being so firm". I played the Old Course at St Andrews on New Year's Day 1971 when the ground was frozen over and rock hard. I reached the green at the par-five 5th hole with a drive and a four-iron. The rest of the round was sub-par, of the sort not normally seen on television.

The green fee was 7/6 (37.5p). I also sliced a ball into the top floor of the Old Course Hotel alongside the 17th hole. I went to a wedding

reception there in December that year, but the
ball hadn't been found.

| *The Times* | **Public school energy bill** | 19 Jul |

Sir, Sir Max Hastings reveals that a big public school
now has an energy bill of £500,000 a year (Notebook,
Jul 19). An increase to a figure still likely to be under
£1000 per pupil would not seem to be significant
when fees are approaching £40,000 a year. It seems
improbable that energy bills alone will cause some
establishments to go bust if the figure quoted is the
right order of magnitude.

| *DTel* | **Boris Johnson's resignation honours list** |

SIR - I much look forward to seeing Boris Johnson's
resignation honours lists - said to be two and
including 30 new peers - in what will surely be his
final act of defiance, or maybe not (Sketch, July 21).

| *The Times* | **Too hot to broadcast** | 21 Jul |

Sir, Discretion being the better part of valour, I spent
Monday and Tuesday indoors, when I came across a
BBC boxset of the complete comedy series *It Ain't Half
Hot, Mum* for sale on ebay. It will liven up sitting out

the next heat wave and I look forward to watching again that particular reflection of the British Army in India (David Aaronovitch, Jul 14, & Letter, Jul 15).

Sunday Times	**Word found**	26 Jul

Phil Whiting is not missing a useful word for his lexicon (Letter, "Lost for Words", last week). What has happened is that the completed Scrabble board must have been set up with "FIGDETS" instead of "FIDGETS", as the G and the D can be interchanged without affecting any other words or the score. An easy mistake to make, no doubt.

The Times	**Celebrations off**	28 Jul

Sir, After the end of the England women's Euro 2022 semi-final against Sweden my wife commented: "Thank goodness they haven't taken their shirts off". I was not so sure.

Wisden Cricket Monthly	*August issue*

The perfect riposte (P)

I too was at The Oval in 1976 on the Saturday of the Test match between

England and the West Indies ['I Was There', Dennis Amiss, WCM57], when a calypso record *Who's Grovelling Now?*, which I still have, was being played and sold around the ground before play started. Thirty years later at a charity event Michael Holding signed the label for me.

This joyful riposte was all that was really necessary off the field of play, and I like to imagine it helped Tony Greig keep in perspective the stick he got for his injudicious remarks.

The Times	**Football heroics**	1 Aug

Sir, History has been made - but surely the Lionesses are heroines not heroes (The Game, "How gutsy heroes vanquished German mentality monsters", Aug 1)?

See also page 224.

The Daily Telegraph *published a letter making this point on 3 Aug 22.*

DTel   **Toby jugs**   5 Aug

SIR - Your caption accompanying the picture of the Boris Johnson Toby Jug ("Poor little kitsch boy", News, August 5) reveals that jugs depicting him have outsold those of Winston Churchill and Margaret Thatcher since he entered No 10 in 2019. This would seem unlikely to continue when Parliament's gift shop online shows that while all the Toby Jugs are Limited editions, those of Margaret Thatcher and Boris Johnson are also Out of Stock. Or, as they are not "Sold Out", are they awaiting the arrival of the next "Limited" editions?

DTel   **Unprecedented**   14 Aug

SIR – Lesley Hall asks if anyone can remember what adjectives we used to describe "unprecedented" occurrences before someone found *unprecedented* (Letters, August 13). I can certainly remember one, which younger readers may not have heard of: *unheard-of*.

Isle of Wight   19 Aug
County Press

Out of date report

Regarding the 365-day licence threat at Ryde.

Your local democracy correspondent has made a reasonable summary of the intentions and objections in regard to the expanded use of the Eastern Gardens in Ryde (CP, 05-8-22) when in the hands of Ryde Town Council (RTC), but her report is now out of date.

Following a meeting of residents of The Strand and representatives of RTC, as well as the posting of representations and objections online, the premises licence application has been withdrawn.

On reapplication, any suggestion that under RTC live music can be played till 11pm, when it is restricted to 8.30pm by the Isle of Wight Council, is likely to be resisted in the strongest terms by nearby residents and others most affected.

Country Life **Vodkatini** 23 Aug

Stirred – Not Shaken (1976) by John Doxat, the first international book about the dry martini, bears out what Jack Banham from Florida in the US holds dear about not shaking, but less so about it 'never (gasp!)' being made with vodka (*Letters, August 17*). Describing non-gin variants as mutations, the author accepts the most popular mutation – a vodkatini – as an acceptable heresy. The foreword (Aperitif) is written by Kingsley Amis, who in his own book *On Drink* published an interesting vodkatini , called Lucky Jim after his famous novel. Made with cucumber juice, Doxat did reckon that this was an instance where shaking might be better than mixing.

DTel **Slash window** 30 Aug

Sir, We have been waiting since February for a purpose-built sash window to be made and fitted to an upper-storey bathroom. Finally put in place earlier this month, the lower window shot up on its own while my sister-in-law was on the loo. On investigation, the top window miraculously closed when opened as well. New weights have since been fitted, but the upper window still shuts when opened and has to be kept ajar with a loo roll. The bottom window won't open as it is now stuck with paint. We await the return of the builder. Gerald Hoffnung's

Bricklayer's Story and *Fawlty Towers'* builders, the O'Reillys, spring to mind.

Stamp Magazine   Sep issue

Colonial confusion

While talking about Stanley Gibbons' purchase of the British Guiana 1856 1c black on magenta, on Radio 4's *World at One* in July, I was astonished to hear Victoria Lajer, the company's Managing Director, referring several times to British Guiana as an island. **Malcolm Watson, Ryde, Isle of Wight (genuinely an island)**

I had copied an email to Ms Lajer to the editor of Stamp Magazine *who published it as the letter above adding* (genuinely an island).

Ms Lajer replied: "Yes, it was an error on my part, I have always been aware it is not an island, it was a simple mistake on my part whilst in conversation with them. No excuses at all, but it has been a very busy day and I've taken a lot of calls."

*Also, Sarah Montague, interviewing her,
thought that a 1st Class stamp cost 76p not
85p.*

The Spectator   **Out with cringe**   2 Sep

Sir: It appears that your Drink columnist, Bruce
Anderson, may not read your letters pages. In the 9
January 2016 edition you published the following
letter from me:

"It will be news to many of those who served with,
or under the command of, the late Field Marshal Sir
Nigel Bagnall that his nickname when out of earshot
was Baggie (Drink, 2 January). Throughout the army
he was referred to as Ginge, on account of his hair.
This is also borne out by the existence of an unofficial
thinktank he convened aside from the chain of
command, but reaching down a rank level or two to
encourage talent for the future. It was known as the
Ginger group by those who may or may not have
been invited to be members of it."

The same applies to 'Baggy', as Anderson now calls
him ('A toast to the field marshals', 3 September).

*PS. If you choose not to publish this, please ensure that
Bruce Anderson receives a copy. They chose not to.*

DTel **England cricket captains** 5 Sep
Sport section

Michael Vaughan is mistaken in saying in his piece
about Joe Root that you captain England only once in
your life (Sport, September 2). In the memories of
many of us, Colin Cowdrey, Mike Brearley, David
Gower and Graham Gooch were all appointed a
second time, though this is unlikely to happen in
Root's case.

Private Eye **Max factor** 5 Sep

The Commentatorballs entry "England really need to
try and get some inertia" (Eye 1579) reminded me of
my tank gunnery instructor imploring us to "use
some mental approach", a factor allegedly affecting
the laying of the aiming mark on the target.

DTel **Pallbearers** 14 Sep

SIR - Major Nigel Price is right to praise the Royal
Regiment of Scotland for their hard work (Letters,
September 14), though those he describes as most
deserving of congratulations were not pallbearers but
the bearer party.

Twelve pallbearers are expected to come from the
ranks of former military staff and be part of the

procession next to the coffin at the state funeral on Monday. The bearer party will be formed by the Grenadier Guards (Picture, page 7, September 13).

Your readers and commentators may like to be reminded of this distinction.

The Times	**Sir Tom Scholar**	14 Sep

Sir, Lord Wilson of Dinton writes unsurprisingly in his Thunderer column (Sep 13) that: "Civil servants will implement whatever the government decides, loyally and with energy, as they always have done", (letter, Sep 14) to counter Lord Agnew's argument and examples of the opposite by the sacked lead permanent secretary at the Treasury, Sir Tom Scholar. The honourable action for someone so found out should be to resign from the civil service and stand for parliament, thus displaying his political inclination and trying his hand that way at determining policy.

The Times	**Young looking**	27 Sep

Sir, May I suggest another group - a bulge even - those born between the end of the Second World War and the birth of the King who now realise how old they are getting (letter, Sep 27). To us, the monarch, for the first time in our lives, looks younger.

Someone else beat me to it with: "One truly appreciates this when popes start to look young".

The Oldie **Hold the front page!** 28 Sep

SIR: It seems improbable that G K Chesterton would have said that the front page of *The Times* was full of long leading articles (Olden Life, October issue). Older readers will recall that the front page of *The Times* was dedicated to advertisements and paid announcements (births, marriage & deaths). It was not until 1966 that the newspaper printed news stories on the front page for the first time, 30 years after the death of the author; leading articles have remained firmly inside.

The Times **Vouching for luncheon vouchers** 1 Oct

Sir, Jane Lambourne's memories of luncheon vouchers valued at 2/6 in 1972 are understandably fond but perhaps a little hazy (letter, 1 Oct). The initial level of 2/3 was increased in 1948 to 3/-. Her 1972 vouchers, converted to decimal currency a year earlier, would have shown a face value of 15p. However, her cheese sandwich and jam doughnut for 15p seems amazing value today; as does five first class stamps that cost 3p each back then.

| *The Times* | **Not Great Yarmouth** | 6 Oct |

Sir, Lest there be any confusion, the opinion of one of Charles Dickens' characters, Peggotty, about "the finest place in the universe" was indeed about Yarmouth (letter, Oct 6), the westernmost town on the Isle of Wight and not Great Yarmouth, the easternmost town in the British Isles, as intimated in the article "Fruit trees banned by Great Yarmouth as health hazard" (online, Oct 5). Interestingly, while Dickens wrote *David Copperfield* in Great Yarmouth, where references to the name are plentiful, a property called "Copperfield" has just been sold near Yarmouth.

| *Country Life* | **Are we really alone** | 6 Oct |

Mark Peaker expresses with some certainty "mankind's inability to comprehend we are alone" (*Letters, October 5*). I am not so sure, preferring to consider the Drake equation, devised in 1961, to estimate the number of active, communicative, extra-terrestrial civilizations in the Milky Way Galaxy. While several of the seven factors in the equation are largely or entirely based on conjecture, their estimation is thought provoking and worth looking into. As well as on Wikipedia, it is covered in Episode 12 of *Cosmos*, the 1980s television series and Chapter 12 of the accompanying book for anyone with access to them.

Daily Telegraph   8 Oct
Sport section

Counties need top players

Joe Root not being available for a key game for Yorkshire in the county championship* is always a disappointment for their members, but last week was not the first time this has happened. In 2016, the final match at Lord's was a chance for Yorkshire to win the championship for the third year running and Root was not allowed to play; at least he was at the ground.

In 2015, Root did not play in a single match for the county's championship-winning side, the team photograph for the record being of a large squad in order to include him it. However the high performance review pans out into a schedule for 2024 and beyond, I sincerely hope that a way can be found for star players to play for their counties in the championship when not on Test match duty.

If it could happen when there were 28 three-day matches, it can surely happen again when there are 14 or fewer four-day matches. The future of first-class/red-ball cricket in this country could depend on it.
Malcolm Watson
(Yorkshire member since 1965)

*Yorkshire lost a must-win match and dropped to the second division of the championship for 2023. The ECB said Root was finished for the year, enabling him to play pro-celebrity golf in Scotland.

DTel	**Scammed**	8 Oct

SIR - I was surprised to read that Lord Butler, Mrs Thatcher's former private secretary, has said that the late prime minister would join him and Sir Philip Moore, the Queen's assistant private secretary, for a debrief after her weekly audience with the late Queen ("William's 'fury' over princes' treatment of former mentor", October 8).

Apart from David Cameron revealing that Her late Majesty purred when he revealed to her the result of the Scottish referendum in 2014, there was me naive enough to believe that what was said between monarch and prime minister stayed between them. Today, it feels as if I have been scammed.

The Times   **Till Death Us Do Part**   10 Oct

Sir, Professor Katie Wales may not know personally anyone who ever found Alf Garnett in *Till Death Us Do Part* to be the "only truly funny" sitcom father-in-law (letter, Oct 10). But judging by the laughter from the live audiences of those must-see early series of the late 1960s, there may well be plenty who did.   I expect there are plenty who still do, who laugh at and not with the reactionary character. John Cleese recently defended the series by pointing out that those who laughed with Alf Garnett were laughed at too.

DTel   **The missing concept**   14 Oct

SIR - Whatever happened to politics being the art of the possible?

The Times   **Avoiding the chop**   14 Oct

Sir, Still nearer Lady Jane Grey's nine days as queen than George Canning's 119 days as prime minister, can Liz Truss avoid the chop? Dear, oh dear.

Liz Truss resigned on 17 Oct 22, 44 days into her tenure. Rishi Sunak became the third Prime Minister in 7 weeks on 25 Oct 22 and the fifth in 7 years.

Private Eye	**Pedantry Corner**	26 Oct

The photograph of Baroness (Natalie) Bennett in military uniform (Eye 1583, p 16) does not show her wearing "camo overalls". She is wearing a two-piece outfit; overalls are one-piece garments. They are generally issued in a single colour to protect clothing underneath, as the name suggests. Now worn with a tweed cap for domestic tasks, my olive-green Army version is the only item of uniform I retained for future use after 39 years' service.

The Times	**Rank outsiders**	27 Oct

Sir, From "the pantheon of victorious rank outsiders" to join the Ireland cricket team (leading article, Oct 27), the 100/1 1967 Grand National winner, Foinavon, would have been a worthy pick after surviving the mêlée at the 23rd fence; perhaps being better known than some of those mentioned, with the fence named after him in 1983.

DTel   **Swapping stamps**   31 Oct

SIR - It is reassuring to read that non-barcoded stamps can still be swapped by Royal Mail after 31 January 2023, their last day of use ("Phase-out of old stamps is 'unfriendly to the elderly'", October 31), a concession not as widely known as it should be. If post offices like the one in Ferndown near Bournemouth are asked 20 times a day to swap stamps, would it not be a friendly gesture if copies of the form needed to change them could be downloaded and provided there by their owners or members of the local community at minimum cost to themselves? The tiny Freepost address would need to be highlighted, but otherwise those inquiring should be able to fill in the form and return it with their stamps for exchange free of charge. Even helpful as well as friendly.

DTel   **Flashing the cash**   1 Nov

SIR - RT Britnell asks why the Government can't target people who need and deserve support instead of spraying cash around to all and sundry purely on the basis of age (Letters, November 1). I suggest it is because the costs of devising and implementing a system to do so will exceed any savings made in the targeting.

Lessons learnt 2 Nov

SIR - Victoria Hawkins rightly questions the inability of the NHS to learn lessons (Letters, October 30). The key to understanding this lies in the terminology.

Lessons must first be identified; a lesson identified should lead to a recommendation; a lesson learnt needs to be accompanied by an action. The benefits come from ensuring that the lessons are actually applied, which is the difficult part, especially when previous decisions are called into question and may need to be overturned, hence "no effective action" being taken.

The NHS, politicians and commentators should refrain from using the expression "lessons have been learnt" unless it is accompanied by descriptions of the lessons and the actions that have been taken; instead, they should learn to use "lessons have been identified" with what has been recommended, when that is all that has happened.

Isle of Wight   4 Nov
County Press

Cut the woke spelling – use capital letters! (P)

I'm not sure about it making the upgrade of
Ryde railway station have a more Victorian
feel (CP, 28-10-22), but a reversion to capital
letters for the proposed name of 'ryde
esplanade' would certainly look more
grown up.

Ryde Esplanade and Coffee are how the
words should appear on the building.

*An article explaining that councillors were
asking for a more Victorian feel to the upgrade of
the station was accompanied by a picture of a
futuristic entrance with a predominance of glass.*

BEER   **Good Beer Guide 2023**   9 Nov
(incorporating
What's Brewing)

I have a copy of the first 49 Good Beer Guides with
their alphabetical listings of pubs by county: nothing
could be simpler to use. For the 50th, the editors have

decided that we need to find the Key Map on page 16, look up the region of the county we are looking for, find the page in the Region Key, go to it and finally get to the county alphabetically – five actions instead of one. It wasn't broken so why fix it? I look forward to the 51st and subsequent editions returning to what has been perfectly satisfactory for 49 years.

PS. The introduction to each region would seem to be unnecessary and an excuse for the grouping by regions.

PPS. Why does 'Public transportation information' suddenly appear at page 201 rather than under 'Indexes & Further Information'?

The Times **Ask for "milts"** 14 Nov

Sir, Herring roes, or "milts", are regularly sold at Waitrose in East Cowes. During my wife's stay in the mainland this week I shall be treating myself to them as described by Mark Lane (letter, Nov 14) using Old Bay Seasoning from the USA , but now available here, in the flour. A staple from my childhood in East Yorkshire, my wife, from much further South, is not so keen.

Waitrose was out of them.

Beaten to it by a correspondent who got hers at Waitrose in Clapham Junction and recommending a hint of Pernod on the toast.

The Times   16 Nov

A cast too far

Sir, Your all-encompassing obituary of David English (Nov 14) contains the wonderful line that he made "an appearance alongside Laurence Olivier, Sean Connery, Robert Redford and Michael Caine in Richard Attenborough's 1977 epic war film *A Bridge Too Far*." I too was an extra in that film, as an unseen crewman in a Sherman tank crossing the bridge at Nijmegen. I shall adopt the same line from now on.

This letter was read out on Times Radio the following Thursday.

Country Life   30 Nov

No thanks for the music

David Lambert says that no fire is probably the most disappointing factor of entering any social room in a hotel or pub *(Letters, November 16)*. Even more disappointing, I would suggest, is piped music – even with a fire.

The Cricketer   December issue

Let Root play (part 2)

Richard Wolfe is mistaken if he thinks there is one rule for the Test ground counties and another for the remainder when it comes to England players playing for their counties (Letters, November). Joe Root was not available for the key game for Yorkshire in the county championship in September and the county has dropped from Division One. Furthermore, this was not the first time that this has happened. In 2016, the final match

at Lord's was a chance for Yorkshire to win
the championship for the third year running
and Root and Jonny Bairstow were not
allowed to play. In 2015, Root did not play
in a single match for the county's
Championship-winning side. By contrast,
in 1966 Yorkshire also had to win their last
match outright, at Harrogate, to be assured
of the title, which they did. Not only did
the home crowd go to see Brian Close, Ray
Illingworth and Geoff Boycott, back after
playing for England in the fifth Test, but
also to watch Colin Cowdrey and the up-
and-coming Derek Underwood (11 wickets
in the match) playing against them for
Kent. I sincerely hope that a way can be
found for England players to play for their
counties when not on Test match duty.

*Two other letters were published on the same
subject either side of mine (parts 1 and 3).
See also page 136 and* Much More Wit and
Wisdom ... *page 51 for a letter to* The Cricket
Paper. *This letter combined the two and was
edited.*

DTel	**Duckett and Roy**	30 Nov

Sport section

Your headline "Duckett given licence to thrill as opener" (Cricket, November 29) is at variance with the text where *thrill* is replaced by *thrive*. Is this the same Test match licence that was given not so long ago to Jason Roy, with predictable failure to do either? As Sir Geoffrey Boycott says on the same page, "he has a lot to prove."

Ben Duckett (107) and Zak Crawley (122) put on 233 for the first wicket in 35.4 overs in the first Test v Pakistan on 1 Dec 22!

DTel	**Out in the midday cold**	1 Dec

SIR - In her article ("We shouldn't be so uneasy about our quirky national customs", December1), Jemima Lewis asks: "Is it seemly (is it even possible?) to say what is distinctively British now?" I suggest that one such custom seems to be grown-ups going around in short trousers in winter. As Noel Coward might have said: "they're obviously definitely nuts!"

Private Eye	**Pedantry Corner**	3 Dec

...David McGillivray says he has waited years "to pedantically correct a pedant" (Pedantry Corner

Special, Eye 1587). Surely a true pedant - one given such special visibility - would not have split an infinitive.

Below the pale

SIR - Charles Moore has made a balanced assessment of the latest saga at the palace (Comment, December 3), but I do hope that something lighter-hearted may eventually emerge from the fallout. Many years ago, I asked facetiously of Margaret Powell, the author of *Below Stairs* (1969) and television personality, during a documentary she was making about The Season, where she had come from. She replied, to much hilarity: "You had better ask my mother that!"

This relates to Lady Susan Hussey asking where palace guest Ngozi Fulani had come from.

and also

Sunday Times **Too brazen?** 7 Dec

Rod Liddle says that every time he meets a stranger he asks them where they are from, because he's nosy and also because he likes guessing accents (Comment, last week).   So do I and I do hope that something lighter-hearted may eventually emerge from the fallout of the latest palace "racism" saga.

Many years ago, I asked facetiously of Margaret Powell, the author of *Below Stairs* (1969) and television personality, during a documentary she was making about The Season, where she had come from. She replied, to much hilarity: "I think you had better ask my mother that!"

Country Life **Orders of Chivalry et al** 8 Dec

R. A. Jones enquires about the sashes, in particular from which shoulder they are hung, and precedence of the orders of chivalry to which they relate (*Letters, 'It's all in the sash', December 7*). In order of precedence: The Most Noble Order of the Garter, The Most Ancient and Noble Order of the Thistle have sashes hung from the left shoulder; The Most Illustrious Order of St Patrick from the right shoulder. Next, in order of precedence: The Most Honourable Order of the Bath, The Most Exalted Order the Star of India, The Most Distinguished Order of St Michael and St George, The Most Eminent Order of the Indian Empire, the Royal Victorian Order and The Most Excellent Order of the British Empire, have sashes hung from the right shoulder on those honoured with the first class of each order. While no one is alive to wear the Orders of St Patrick, the Star of India or the Indian Empire, many portraits, photographs and footage from films exist of those so honoured in the past wearing their sashes over the appropriate shoulder. As to when they are worn today, occasions designated 'ceremonial' or 'white tie' will probably cover it.

Incidentally, John F. Mueller (*'A point of honour', November 9*) is mistaken in saying that there is a female counterpart to Knight Bachelor. The lowest knightly honour that can be conferred on a woman is the Dame Commander of the Order of the British Empire, one rank higher than the Knight Bachelor. Dames in the highest class of the Orders of the Bath, St Michael and St George, the Royal Victorian Order and the Order of the British Empire also wear (narrower) sashes hung from the right shoulder.

Resubmitted as a shorter version omitting the dormant Orders of St Patrick, the Star of India and the Indian Empire, it was published on 11 Jan 23 with the second paragraph omitted. *See page 155.*

| *DTel* | **Abandoned principles** | 10 Dec |

SIR - In her different take on the Duke and Duchess of Sussex ("Trust me, this is the real Harry and Megan we're seeing at last", December 10), Bryony Gordon says that she met "the principles" at County Hall in London. It was of course "the principals" that she met; the couple seem to have abandoned their principles.

DTel   **Well done British Gas!**   21 Dec

SIR - After reading all the correspondence about British Gas this week, it was with some trepidation that I rang them. The call was answered quickly and I was put though, via a crackly line, to what must have been a call centre. I confirmed my details, gave a reading, closed an account and opened it again in a different name, all within 10 minutes. I was rung back and asked how they had done: I gave them full marks on their short survey, the type I usually decline to answer.

2023

The Times   **Vowels unblocked**   3 Jan

Sir, Huw Benyon recalling the challenge of writing a paragraph , or even a decent sentence, without the letter E (letter, Jan 2) had me scrabbling for details I had printed off about a book in which each of its five chapters uses only one vowel. Called *Eunoia* (2001) - the shortest word in English containing all five vowels and meaning 'beautiful thinking' - it was written by Canadian poet Christian Bok and a British edition was published in 2008. The author believed "his book proves that each vowel has its own personality, and demonstrates the flexibility of the English language." The postscript of the book says that each chapter uses at least 98% of the available words. Its 112 pages sold well enough in the UK to make The Times list of the year's top 10 books that Christmas.

Letters were published on 3 Jan commending La Disparisian *(1969) and* Gadsby *(1939). A shortened version of the one above on* Eunoia *was resubmitted but beaten to it by another correspondent on 4 Jan.*

DTel   **The Sussexes and the Coronation**   10 Jan

SIR - Loved by many of her subjects but hated by her husband, Westminster Abbey's door was slammed in Queen Caroline's face when she attempted to attend King George IV's Coronation in 1821. If the Duke of

Sussex is not reconciled with his father and brother by the time of his father's Coronation in May (Leading article, January 10), then it could conceivably be the public that prevents the Duke and Duchess of Sussex getting anywhere near that abbey door this time.

A full article on the subject of the 1821 Coronation was published opposite the letters pages the next day, supporting and giving full context to my point.

Country Life   11 Jan

Wear it right (P)

R. A. Jones enquires about the sashes, in particular from which shoulder they are hung, and precedence of the British orders of chivalry to which they relate (*Letters, 'It's all in the sash', December 7*). In order of precedence: the Order of the Garter and the Order of the Thistle have sashes hung from the left shoulder. Next, the Order of the Bath, the Order of St Michael and St George, the Royal Victorian Order and the Order of the British Empire have sashes hung from the right shoulder on those honoured with the first class of each order.

As to when they are worn today, occasions designated 'ceremonial' or 'white tie' will probably cover it.

For a fuller version, see page 149.

Daily Telegraph   19 Jan

Marmalade mixer

SIR - While marmalade can indeed be made with blood oranges (Letters, January 18), for the best of both worlds use Seville oranges with Blood Orange Cointreau. *I provide the liqueur for ours.*

Italics omitted.

The Times   **Not easy to say surnames**   21 Jan

Sir, As far as counterintuitive pronunciation of surnames is concerned (letter, Jan 21), Leveson-Gower – pronounced Lewson-Gore – must take some beating.

Featherstonehaugh had been mentioned.

The Spectator **AI rewards** 22 Jan

Sir: The concept of a computer having a letter published in the *Spectator* is an intriguing one (Letters, 21 January). However, to win a bottle of Pol Roger the computer would need to 'read' and inwardly digest an article in *Country Life* magazine, additionally being able to 'interpret' colour photographs and other illustrations, before winning the Letter of the Week – a significant step up. Perhaps the bottle could be sent to a human runner-up.

Daily Telegraph 30 Jan

Tasteful tequila

SIR – I was amused to read that clear tequila is regarded as posh by "high-end huns*" (Features, January 26).

When living in Mexico in the late 90s, I discovered early on that clear tequila is the working man's drink, consumed in tumblers with sparkling grapefruit and in copious quantities to keep refreshed at outdoor events. One marque, Herradura Blanco, which at 46% ABV was not for export, attracted the opprobrium "para los hombres"; though I met the Mexican wife of a British expat who drank it neat as her pre-lunch tipple.

Huns are best described as over-50 ladettes.

The Spectator	**Stamps without barcodes**	30 Jan

Sir: Mary Killen not need worry that, come 31 July, "we will have no choice but to go with the barcoded versions of stamps" which Royal Mail have rolled out (Notes on..., 'Stamps', 28 January). Non-barcoded Christmas themed stamps will continue to be valid, as will all Special Stamps, which are not to be barcoded. There will be 14 more issues of Special Stamps during 2023, including those to commemorate the new reign of King Charles III on the day of his coronation, 6 May. These pictorial stamps are offered less for postage than they should be. Being free of barcodes could be just the boost they need from those still having reason to use snail mail, but remember to ask for them.

Another letter was published referring to the same article, but on a different aspect of it.

The Times   **Beer robbery**   6 Feb

Sir, £1.79 a pint! Absolute robbery. Wetherspoon's pubs have just put their January sale price of 99p a pint up to £1.71 (letter, Feb 6).

Country Life   **But which butter is the best?**   6 Feb

Sally Kellard is clear as to what she regards as the best items required for guests to savour buttered toast, but her letter (*February 1*) still begs the question: 'Which is the best butter?' For me it would be one of those that contains sea-salt crystals.

Private Eye   ***Spare***   9 Feb

In terms of your take on the incendiary memoir 'Spare' as 'Spart' ("The King of Troubles", Eye 1571) and its tawdry revelation about Prince Harry's loss of virginity, perhaps 'Spurt' would be more appropriate. Or was it a typo?

The Ed says: Many thanks for taking the time to send this to us.

The Times **Peers' coronation robes** 10 Feb

Sir, It seems a pity that the need for peers to wear ceremonial robes at the coronation is being scrapped (Royal family, thetimes.co.uk, Feb 9). Brought in for the coronation of King George IV, these flowing robes indicate the rank of the peer by the number of rows of ermine tails on the miniver cape along with associated coronet, helping commentators, one would hope, identify those in Westminster Abbey for a worldwide audience. Perhaps peers with key roles in the ceremony with still wear theirs, otherwise it seems that these coronation robes will only be seen in a few historic houses where they are on display.

On 3 May it was announced that coronation robes could be worn by those attending, but without coronets.

DTel **Black and white cars** 14 Feb

SIR - When serving in the army in West Berlin in the early 80s, I had the use of a small black staff car. It was then replaced by a white one - I assumed because they were cooler to travel in during the hot summer months. Not a bit of it: white cars fetched higher prices than black ones when auctioned off.

Correspondence about colours of cars had been going on for 5 days when I tried to join in.

The Times **Twinned with graffiti** 14 Feb

Sir, I remember the late Arthur Marshall saying on the television show *Call My Bluff* that a sign near where he lived in Devon had beneath it "twinned with Profiteroles" (letter, Feb 14).

A number of letters had been published giving favourite graffito, including one offering "twinned with Pommes de Terre".

The Times **Bettys' apostrophes** 17 Feb

Sir, Janice Turner (born 1964) would not have made her faux pas calling a Fat Rascal a Fat Bastard in Betty's café (notebook, Feb 16; letter, Feb 17). Rather, her faux pas was including the apostrophe, which the tea rooms dropped in 1965.

DTel **Sandwich fillings** 22 Feb

SIR - Christine Baldock's classification of sandwich fillings (Letters, February 22) fits my own childhood recollections: demerara sugar with brown bread, dripping with white.

A correspondent had offered sweet fillings with brown bread, savoury with white. Subsequent suggestions offered examples of the opposite.

Sunday Times **You say** 26 Feb
Culture section

Donna Francis is too young to have seen **Crown Court** (Talking Pictures) first time around. I can't watch the actor Richard Wilson without seeing him as the youthful Jeremy Parsons QC. The jury were not actors, but made up from members of the public.

The Times **Queuing for fun** 27 Mar

Sir, Early morning queues for theatre tickets were not the only ones where fun could be found (letter, March 27). The mid-winter one-day sales of shirts and ties at Turnbull & Asser's Jermyn Street store in the 70s were splendid social occasions. Patiently awaiting the store to open, the queue grew steadily down Bury Street, kept warm by complimentary coffee provided by the nearby restaurant, Quaglino's - in china cups and saucers, of course.

The Spectator **Beaten to the challenge** 11 Apr

Sir: Bruce Anderson weaves into his column (April 8) the notable London restaurants The Guinea Grill and Bellamy's in Bruton Street. It seems unlikely that Bellamy's would take up the challenge of producing a succulent pie (however 'damn fine' it might be), when

The Guinea - renowned for its award-winning pies – has four on its menu already.

The Oldie   **Careless captions**   11 Apr

SIR: I was relishing the prospect of reading about some marvellous mistakes made at the 1953 Coronation (Right royal blunders, by Hugo Vickers, May issue), when two howlers leapt out from the pages. The main photograph shows the Queen, not with St Edward's Crown, but with the Imperial State Crown; and the caption for the photograph of the scene in the Abbey has the Queen with her 'ladies-in-waiting', when the text correctly describes them as her maids of honour.

I can only imagine what Hugo Vickers thinks.

Sunday Times   **Postage stamp prices**   12 Apr

Your informative Chart of the Week ("More than a pound to post a letter", Money, last week) was inaccurate in adding that stamps were 1p when they first came into use in 1840: they cost 1d then, less than one seventh of the 3p charged for a first-class stamp in 1971. Prior to decimalisation there were 240d in £1.

DTel **Jeans** 22 Apr

SIR - Shirley Horwich is indeed not unique in never having owned a pair of jeans (Letters, April 22). I did though acquire in the USA a pair of blue denim Dockers cut with conventional pockets. These I wear for charity on occasions when asked to come in denim.

The Times **Knocking it back** 29 Apr

Sir, Following Brian Empringham's lead (letter, Apr 29), I have dunked a ginger nut in a newly launched Coronation Spritz made with gin, rose lemonade and King's Ginger. Nothing to knock there.

He had suggested that the only place to dunk a ginger nut was not in tea, but in a gin and tonic; and not to knock it until you tave tried it.

DTel **Cricket in August** 30 Apr
Sport section

Nick Hoult, Chief Cricket Correspondent, is mistaken in saying that the Hundred will be the only cricket played in England in August (Cricket, April 29). In addition to 34 days' worth of the Hundred, there are 72 50-over matches in the One-Day Cup, as well as the quarter- and semi-finals, all to be played in

August between first-class counties. Lest we forget, this is a format in which we are world champions. I should add that four of the matches are to be played in Wales, as are four days of the Hundred.

Stamp Magazine   May issue

A gap in the market for someone to fill?

Your recent editorial comment (March issue, page 4) about scanning a treasured collection to preserve a record of it for posterity reflected my own thinking.

Unfortunately, of the seven albums I would wish to copy, only two have pages that are removable. The others are bound-in pages, making the scanning a heavy and clumsy task.

I would still like to do this , but the prospect is not one I relish.

I wonder if there is someone in the philatelic market who is offering to undertake this kind of work? Or whether it is an opportunity for someone to take up?

This letter was reworked by the editor from an email I sent him personally about my enquiry.

DTel   **Frugal chairs**   1 May

SIR - It is understandable that the King wants chairs used at previous coronations to be repaired and reused for his Coronation on Saturday. Though "gilding and furniture restorers have cleaned, restored and consolidated the giltwood frames" of the Chairs of Estate, the frames illustrated show the monogram of the late Prince Philip and an E for the late Queen still place. (Front page picture and News, May 1). It really would be frugal if they stayed that way for Saturday.

DTel   2 May

Coronation spectacle

SIR - How right Judith Woods is that we are being deprived of the spectacle we crave on Coronation Day (Features, April 28).

Those wanting to see - or remind themselves of - what such a spectacle looks like should seek out the award-winning documentary *A Queen is Crowned* (1953) narrated by Laurence Olivier. It is available on YouTube and lasts for 79 minutes.

Other letters under the heading concerned the inappropriateness of the public oath-taking and having neighbours around for a glass of fizz in the garden.

Country Life   3 May

Tottering over the limit

How I sympathised with Dr Chris Godfrey (*Letters, April 19*) in his pursuit of matching the tasting notes to the bottle of Chardonnay you had recommended (*Notebook, March 29*) and his downing of the bottle. Expecting that he was a doctor of medicine, I recalled the conversation Lord Tottering had had with his doctor (*Tottering-by-gently, January 10, 2018*): 'And do you adhere to the 14 units of alcohol limit recommended for men?' 'I'm not sure doctor, some days "yes", some days "no."'

(Dr Godfrey may, of course, be a doctor of geology).

The £6 bottle of Chardonnay from Morrisons had been described as having '...a spiced nose of pineapple and creamy custard tart. Melon and citrus flavours, textured and buttery peach, balanced by mineral acidity. More yellow fruits and grapefruit on the long finish. Excellent value.'

Isle of Wight   5 May
Observer

Mistaken identity (P)

Dear Editor,
Sally Wright is mistaken about a Tony Hancock sketch (Island soapbox, Apr 29). It was Kenneth Williams as Julius Caesar in the film *Carry On Cleo* (1964) that uttered the line 'Infamy, infamy, they've all got it in for me!'. It has been voted as one of the all-time funniest one-liner jokes in a film.

The Times **Smoking cigars** 5 May

Sir, Four peers have declared that all smoking is harmful and addictive (letter, May 5). I suggest that it depends on what is smoked and when it started. I took up smoking cigars while the non-resident defence attaché in Havana when I was 49. Now 75 and used to the time-honoured tradition of celebrating events with a cigar, I have never smoked cigarettes, nor inhaled while smoking cigars. I do not envisage becoming addicted, or dying from cancer as a result of my indulgence. I shall be celebrating the Coronation with a couple of cigars over the weekend - outdoors, of course. I sincerely hope that others will be able to do likewise at the next coronation, whether I am able to join them or not.
Malcolm Watson
Colonel (retd)

DTel **Real men...** 5 May

SIR - *Real Men Don't Cook Quiche* (1983) either – they thaw.

A correspondent had alerted readers to the book Real Men Don't Eat Quiche *in response to the poorly received recipe for Coronation quiche.*

DTel   **National Trust and the Coronation**   8 May

SIR - I was surprised and disappointed to find that
the National Trust has not offered any items to mark
the Coronation; staff at their shops and online were
unable to explain why. By contrast, a number of
tasteful china mugs were produced for them to mark
significant birthdays of the late Queen Mother, then
the trust's President. It seems particularly odd, even
disrespectful, that no commemorative items have
been for sale when the King has been the trust's
President since the death of his grandmother. I am
hoping to discover why this is the case, but I am not
holding my breath.

DTel   **Line of succession – the Spare** 12 May

SIR-Judith Woods describes Prince Louis as the Spare
(Features, "Lay off Prince Louis and let the poor little
lad just be", May 12). Not anymore. Since the
Succession to the Crown Act (2013) ended male
primogeniture and came into force in March 2015,
Princess Charlotte retained her position as the Spare
on the birth of their brother Prince Louis. Indeed, just
let him be.

DTel   **Stress relievers**   16 May

SIR - Higher than taking exams on most lists of
stressful events is moving house (Letters, May 16).
Having done so 13 times, our routine at the end of a
hard day included announcing that it was time for
some 'stress relievers'. These took the form of a large
gin and tonic - preferably made with duty-free
export-strength gin - and worked wonderfully well.

Sunday Times   **Self-publish and be damned**   28 May

I cannot agree with Camilla Long (Comment, May 28)
that novels debuting the characters John Self (Martin
Amis) and Rupert Campbell-Black (Jilly Cooper)
"could never, ever, be written now". Of course they
could: what the authors might struggle with is to find
a publisher. But self-publishing is available today
and any such budding authors should not be afraid to
use it.

DTel   **Internet shopping**   29 May

SIR - Janice Spencer (Letters, May 27) says that you
can't treat yourself to coffee and cake after shopping
on the internet. You can do better that, eating and
drinking whatever you like during internet shopping,
as well as afterwards. Men do not go shopping, but
go out to make specific purchases, moving on as

quickly as possible to the next one, before returning home. I find this is best now done on the internet, whether from a PC, laptop or mobile phone. Returns and refunds have been honoured - I'll drink to that.

Isle of Wight   2 Jun
County Press

Savings make it worthwhile

Clair Allan is mistaken in intimating that Wightlink do not offer discounts for ferry travel for Island residents (CP 29-05-23), but you have to purchase tickets in advance.

If she and husband were able to buy 10 ferry tickets at £330, they could make their return journey to the New Forest for £66 (rather than £292 quoted) and still have four more return journeys to enjoy *from Yarmouth, or Fishbourne,* in the 12 months after purchase.

They could also offer them to their family for their use too.

Red Funnel is best for day-return trips which are available for around £45.

Both companies offer reductions for foot passengers for Senior Citizens (60+) and up to seven passengers per vehicle at no extra cost.

I appreciate that not everyone has £330 to pay up front, but the savings to be made do make it worthwhile if a way can be found to do so.

Italics omitted.

The Spectator   **Six reigns at age 64**   4 Jun

Sir: Anne Fisher says that being 91, she has lived through five reigns (Letters, 3 June). My grandparents all lived during six reigns, the first to die, in 1957, was only 64. Being born in the same year as the present King, I might see a fourth reign. The run-up to this Coronation saw much talk of a once-in-a-generation (25 years) event, but that was never so. The number of reigns and coronations lived through depends solely on one's dates of birth and death.

DTel   **The beer escalator**   4 Jun

SIR - Last year, I reported on the £6.10 pint of beer at Headingley (Letters, 1 July 2022). At Lord's Cricket

Ground, for the first Test match of the season, the price of a pint of beer has now reached £7; a craft version was also on sale at £7.50. Will these prices be beaten at The Oval? We'll find out next week.

DTel **Marmite beaten by Bovril** 12 Jun

SIR - Enough about Marmite! Bovril is the real deal, spreads easily and follows the butter into the holes in toasted crumpets.

Incidentally, at my boarding school in the 1950s (Letters, June 10,12), the novelty was to beat a portion of Marmite with a knife until the colour disappeared, which also made it spread more easily.

DTel **MoD procurement culture** 18 Jun

SIR - I read with more than a passing interest of the damning report into Britain's £5bn Ajax fighting vehicles project (Business, June 16) being more than 10 years late and that "Some individuals showed a clear desire to solve problems at their level, and not bother leaders unless strictly necessary...elevating problems was a sign of failure."

I was involved in the 1990s with the successful procurement of Challenger 2 tanks for the British Army and Desert Warrior fighting vehicles for export. Initiative and determination have always been employed and encouraged to overcome problems at levels where the expertise lies, but if they couldn't be, then they were elevated early using the maxim that those with higher level responsibility are prepared to handle bad news, but don't like surprises.

This independent report looks like bad news, but should not be a surprise.

Colonel JMC Watson (retd)

Country Life   **Panamas for ladies**   27 Jun

The sea of Panama hats at Wimbledon - all with black bands - accompanying the informative article (*'Let it go to your head', June 21*) looks rather bland compared to those often on display at Lord's, where coloured bands abound and on ladies' heads as well. The bows for ladies' Panama hats are sown on to the rear rather than the left side of the hats, along with tails to add a certain flourish. Shown worn by my three daughters at a Test match, they are suitable for summer racing meetings as well but, traditionally of course, not before Glorious Goodwood.

The publication of this letter on 5 July will be included in the next volume, Still More Wit and Wisdom of an Ordinary Subject.

At which point the fifth packet of Wit and Wisdom letters ends.

TRAVEL

TRAVEL TOPICS

During the period covered the letters in *The Daily Telegraph* Saturday *Travel* section disappeared, followed by those in *The Sunday Telegraph Travel* section as well. After a short email correspondence, the requests for tips and recommendations on a specified topic frequently related to a feature article that week, reappeared in the Saturday *Travel* section. Entries are limited to 150 words and the winning review gets a prize.

In the meantime the *Sunday Times* continues with letters in its own *Travel* section, though most of them are now taken from comments made on its online version. There is no limit on the number of words, though entries generally contain many fewer than 150.

What follows are all the entries submitted, with those published shown in a larger font. They are shown in the format published, with the headings and subscripts as used in each. As with the other letters, (P) indicates that the published entry was accompanied by a photograph.

| *Sunday Times* | **Ascension Island** | 28 Oct 20 |

Chris Haslam notes ("Deadly cost of Africa's 'shutdown'", last week) that the Foreign Office advises against non-essential travel to all but three of Africa's 54 nations – Ascension, Mauritius and the Seychelles. However, Ascension Island is not actually one of those 54 – it is part of the United Kingdom Overseas Territory of St Helena, Ascension, and Tristan da Cunha. St Helena and Tristan de Cunha are also exempt from the non-essential travel restrictions. Getting to them could provide just the challenge for those wanting more than a staycation, not least because commercial flights to and from St Helena (see also last week) and Ascension are limited and there is no flight access to Tristan da Cunha. Go to it readers! (Or there is still the Isle of Wight.)

Sunday Telegraph   17 Jan 21
Travel on Sunday

The holiday that taught you the most

KYOTO PROTOCOL

In April 1970, I was in Osaka, Japan, for five unforgettable days at Expo '70. It gave me a chance to learn about the temples and gardens of Kyoto, the etiquette of the bathhouse, and the fact that the Japanese drive on the left – a surprise to me. With 95 countries exhibiting at the fair and a further 32 themed pavilions, this site was filled with discoveries.

One highlight was a large moon rock on display in the US pavilion, brought back by Apollo 12 astronauts in 1969. I saw there the first-ever IMAX film and demonstrations of early mobile phones, local area networking, magnetic levitation (maglev) train technology and electric cars – all now familiar to today's travellers.

STel   **On the road again**   9 Feb 21

After lockdown I plan to continue my quest to play golf on the 18-hole courses at the extremities of Great Britain and Ireland. Already in the bag are the most southerly course, Mullion in Cornwall; and the most westerly, Ceann Sibéal on the Dingle Peninsula in Ireland. To be conquered are the Reay Golf Club on the north coast of Scotland and Gorleston Golf Club on the east coast of Norfolk.

My road-trip will also take in days at the races on the similarly located racecourses of Great Britain. Keen race goers are often surprised to find that they are: most southerly, Newton Abbot, westerly, Ayr; northerly, Perth; easterly, Great Yarmouth.

After playing golf in Cornwall in sunshine and in Ireland in fierce wind, I expect to come across extreme weather conditions in my quest. The thirteen-year-old Renault Espace should have room for all the clothing and equipment needed to cope.

STel **Memories of Scarborough** 23 Feb 21

My teenage years between 1961 and 1966 were spent at the Scarborough Cricket Festival seeing all the tourists from Richie Benaud's Australians to Garry Sobers' West Indians, plus England's and Yorkshire's stars of that era. At the sound of gunfire from the re-enactment of the Battle of the River Plate at nearby Peasholm Park, Freddie Trueman used to pretend to have been shot. A budget of £2 a day provided for food and other entertainment at the cinema, two theatres with summer shows and an outdoor theatre with another musical extravaganza. Sunday was a rest day for the players then, which enabled us to drop down onto the South Bay via the funicular to the beach and other amusements. I plan to visit the ground in July when Yorkshire play Lancashire, 60 years on from my first visit, watch that battle and ride once again on the North Bay miniature railway.

Sunday Telegraph   5 Apr 21
Travel on Sunday

Scottish travel secrets

ART DECO ADORATION

Twenty-one years ago I was on a solo trip to Glasgow and discovered the art deco splendour of restaurant Rogano at 11 Exchange Place. Fashioned on the liner Queen Mary built on the city's Clyde docks, its wonderful vintage lettering and red illuminated sign draw you in to a choice of sitting at the oyster bar, Café Rogano, or the restaurant under the ceiling of deco coloured glass.

Famed for the luxury and elegance of its fish and seafood dishes, it also offered afternoon tea. I chose the café, a more informal venue with its brasserie dishes, to taste and enjoy my very first haggis. Serving Glaswegians since 1935, it closed its doors last year amid the Covid-19 pandemic, but it is hoped that following refurbishment it will reopen sometime in

2021. If you have the opportunity, visit this gem when it does.

Sunday Telegraph   13 Jun 21
Travel on Sunday

Favourite beach

SAFE HAVEN

Sitting at the edge of the Belize Barrier Reef, Goff's Caye is one of the country's few small islands that is not privately owned. Just a 30-minute boat ride from Belize City, you will discover unspoiled beauty, a powdery white sand beach and aquamarine waters make the perfect getaway for people of all ages – *simply lie under the natural shade of the palm trees.*

Children can play on the beach and in the shallow waters yet never be out of sight. Snorkelling can be done safely from the shore, with plenty to see *for first-timers.* Further out, in a maximum of 15 feet of water, there are large colourful coral formations and numerous ocean creatures to see, including lionfish and barracuda.

There is a small hut for cooking and shelter, plus another with a couple of loos. This place really is fantastic.

Italics edited out.

Sunday Telegraph   4 Jul 21
Travel on Sunday

Caribbean islands

A RUM DEAL

You won't be flying to Barbados on Coconut Airways of the 1975 song by Typically Tropical, but Coconut Car Rentals can provide you with reliable and affordable vehicles once there. We hired one *to get to the more remote parts of the island like the rugged east coast, the north point and the most southerly beach at Silver Sands. We made a special effort* to explore the lush interior where much of the island's true beauty can only be appreciated through treks, tours or hill climbs through such rarely visited parishes as St Thomas and St George.

The signature tour at the Mount Gay Rum Visitor Centre provided best value: it covers the history of rum, its production and five rum tastings. We returned with a fridge magnet mapping the 11 *administrative* parishes – useful for pub quizzes – Christ Church being the only one not named after a Saint.

Italics omitted from the published version, which we did explore, rather than the interior which we didn't.

STel	**USA – big drives**	5 Jul 21

We drove from Mexico City to Washington DC in November 2000, taking nine days from Laredo on the Texas border. We found the Old San Francisco Steakhouse in San Antonio, seeing the girl on a swing above the bar ring bells on the ceiling. Via Houston and on to cross the Mississippi at Natchez. Made to shelter in the Visitor Centre, we saw next day giant oak trees beside the scenic Natchez Trace Parkway flattened by a tornado. The trace/trail roughly follows a historic corridor used by American Indians and European settlers. At Chattanooga, Tennessee, the Choo Choo Hotel offers rooms in railway carriages. The Christmas decoration season underway, nowhere was it more evident than in the style of an English country house at the Vanderbilts' Biltmore Estate in North Carolina. The final stretch took us over the Blue Ridge Mountains in Virginia. Blow-out: Chesapeake Bay blue crabs on arrival.

Sunday Telegraph   29 Aug 21
Travel on Sunday

North of England

BOARD AND LODGING

One year we took my mother and her identical twin sister to Swinton Park, a luxury castle hotel in North Yorkshire, to celebrate their 80th birthdays. Evacuated there during the Second World War from their boarding school in Harrogate, the sisters showed me a photograph from December 1939 of girls – including one of the twins – descending a staircase.

We had a spacious private dining room where we had lunch and they recalled their time there, describing their dormitory in the turret, which was now a guest bedroom. These were early days of the Swinton Estate opening the castle to the public and we have watched with interest as the enterprise has diversified and appear on *Amazing Hotels: Life Beyond The Lobby.*

Whether it is enrolling on a cookery course, enjoying a quiet stay, exploring the outdoor space, or celebrating, this is a place for lasting memories.

Sunday Telegraph   2 Oct 21
Travel on Sunday

Rediscovering America

AMAZING ARIZONA

Of the 38 contiguous States of the USA I visited while living there for three years, the one I love was Arizona – and I intend to explore it further. Beyond the dramatic beauty of the Grand Canyon and Monument Valley lies country that is more mountainous than Switzerland, has more sunshine than Florida, more Parks and National Monuments than any other state, and the largest Indian population in the US owning nearly 27% of the land.

From its southern border, it is just 60 miles to the beaches of Mexico on the Gulf of California. However, it is the novelty of skiing there – in one of four resorts that offer 30 miles of slopes – that I'd most like to experience now.

My 38 states were changed (amongst other editing) to 48 in print. My own editing seems not to have left it clear that of the 48 contiguous states I had visited 38 of them.

STel   **Favourite autumn destination**   4 Oct 21

SKYLINE DRIVE, USA

Every autumn, Northern Virginia produces just about
the most spectacular show of fall foliage to appear
anywhere in the world. More than 95% of the
Shenandoah National Park's 190,000 acres are
wooded – groups of hardwood (oak, hickory, maple)
that explode into colour during the first short, cold
days of autumn. Ninety minutes motoring from
Washington DC, the 105-mile Skyline Drive – 80 miles
of it on the spine of the Blue Ridge Mountains – is
simply stunning. It is an unparalleled leaf-viewing
experience, with shades varying from green to yellow,
then red/purple and then brown, seen from above the
beautiful valley of the Shenandoah River. With
numerous stops and overlooks, you don't even need
to leave the comfort of your vehicle. But check
the weather first, then go on the less populous
weekdays and allow at least four hours. It is worth
every cent of the $25 vehicle entry fee.

Sunday Times   **Rothenburg**   12 Oct 21

Rothenburg is much more than the honeypot of the
road ("Romance of the open road", last week). It is
the best preserved example of a medieval town in
Germany, which overlooks the steep, beautiful
Tauber River valley. Still a typical 16th-century town,

its gabled houses have retained their steep Gothic roofs and oriel windows. Its huge encircling fortress walls and watchtowers are straight out of a fairy tale. The town inside the walls is intriguingly medieval as well, with its countless narrow cobblestone streets and graceful flowing fountains, beckoning you to explore the shops, restaurants, taverns and museums. It is a great place to spend at least one night.

Sunday Telegraph   5 Dec 21
Travel on Sunday

Unusual travel experiences

ON TO A WINNER

In *August 1970 in* Cyprus, a local chicken farmer and I helped crew a ketch from Kyrenia to Beirut in exchange for flights back to Nicosia. Over three days we visited the temple ruins at Baalbeck, *Lebanon's greatest Roman treasure;* viewed the stunning underground crystallized caves of Jelia Grotto by boat, and relaxed over a meal at Byblos harbour, where the walls of the restaurant displayed photographs of visiting Hollywood stars.

The night before leaving, we went to the Casino du Liban, where it was said at the time to offer the greatest show on earth. The cabaret included not only dolphins swimming in a huge tank on stage, but horses and riders also displayed their skills and, confirming the hype, elephants too.

We left a chaotic Beirut airport and learnt next day that the Foreign Office had advised against travelling to *the* Lebanon.

Italics omitted, as were any dates to other published experiences, about which they had "had some amazing responses."

Daily Telegraph   21 Mar 22
Travel section

British legacy lives on

ROYAL TREATMENT

You won't see a "bobby" on every corner, but you will find *red letterboxes*, red double-decker buses, afternoon tea at the ivy-clad Empress Hotel, and cricket in Beacon Hill

Park *and three challenging, scenic golf courses.* For this is *the beautiful city of* Victoria on Vancouver Island, the capital of British Columbia and the most British city in Canada.

Further evidence *of its British connection* shows in its Victorian architecture, including the stately Legislative buildings and the palatial Craigdarroch Castle built by [a Scottish immigrant who made his fortune in coal] *a coal baron for his Scottish wife.* For plant enthusiasts, *the city's number one attraction, the world-class* Butchart Gardens includes an English garden abundant with rose beds, *arches* and arbours. *It is a centre for year-round competitive sailing and cruising, plus a launch spot for whale-watching.*

With the Royal London Wax Museum and its chamber of horrors also on hand, you will never feel more at home when abroad.

Italics omitted; square brackets inserted.

DTel **Newhaven harbour** 19 Apr 22

For those of us brought up a day-trip away, the joys of Scarborough with its fine sandy beaches never included swimming in the sea, which was far too cold for comfort. For that we were lucky enough to be taken as children in the summers of the early 1960s to the south coast, where it is warmer. The trouble there though is the beaches, or rather, the lack of sand. The popular ones at Bournemouth, Brighton and Eastbourne are pebble beaches and uncomfortable to sit and walk on. This conundrum was solved by our mother taking us to a wonderful hotel inland on the South Downs Way. On sunny days, we travelled to the shelter of Newhaven harbour with its fine sandy beach. There we enjoyed the opportunity to swim without trepidation on entering the sea, or shivering on getting out, a far cry from the cold North Sea.

DTel **Munich beerless but peerless** 5 Sep 22

Much of the city was destroyed in bombing raids during World War II, but unlike some sister cities, Munich eschewed the modern and reconstructed its past. In some cases, original plans were used to rebuild or restore its landmarks. Todays' public buildings reflect the styles in which they were built over the centuries: late Gothic, Venetian Renaissance, Neoclassical, Rococco and Baroque. Church spires and bell towers, rather than high-rise office buildings, dominate the skyline. Munich has a perfectly integrated system of buses, trams, and subways to help you enjoy the city, including: the Deutsches Museum, the largest museum of science and technology in the world; the 18th century English Garden, one of the oldest landscaped parks on the continent; Schloss Nymphenburg, a prince's gift to his wife for the birth of an heir; then for completeness, two modern landmarks, the 1972 Olympic Village and the Gasteig Cultural Centre.

Daily Telegraph   1 Oct 22
Travel section

City break secrets

THE ONLY WAY IS UPP…

The university (founded in 1477) and cathedral city of * Uppsala lies less than 40 miles north of Stockholm and offers much of historic interest to make a day trip worthwhile. In addition to the medieval cathedral and fine 17th-century castle, the famous silver Bible, Codex Argenteus, is housed in the university library; Swedish botanist Carolus Linnaeus is honoured with a museum at his former house; and burial mounds represent the only Viking remains in this part of Sweden.

Soak up the atmosphere as you down Viking-style mead served in traditional ornamental horns at pubs like the Odinsborg Café & Restaurant nearby. On the way to Uppsala, a short detour will take you to the oldest town in Sweden, Sigtuna. *This small community was once immensely important, serving as the capital of the nation for over a century.**

Italics omitted. A second published entry about a trip I have not actually made but only read about, when visiting Stockholm in 2014.

Daily Telegraph   29 Oct 22
Travel section

Travels in Latin America

MEXICO FURTHER

Oaxaca in southern Mexico is a gem of a colonial city offering 16th-century architecture, magnificent churches, excellent museums, a colourful outdoor market and fascinating side trips to archaeological ruins and indigenous villages. Most impressive is Monte Albán, just six miles south-west, once an important Zapotec and Mixtec religious city with more than 50,000 inhabitants; now one of the country's most impressive archaeological sites consisting of a central hilltop plaza, various buildings, ball courts and more than 150 tombs. Covering 25 square miles, its occupation dates from 900 BC to its decline around 1300 AD.

Before returning to Oaxaca stop in Santa Maria de Tule to see a natural wonder: the famous Tule tree, a giant ahuehuete cypress about 140 feet high, 190 feet around the trunk and still growing. It is estimated to be between 2,500 and 3,200 years old, making it very likely the oldest tree in the world.

DTel   **Unesco World Heritage Sites**   11 Dec 22

Guanajuato is a charming, picturesque, perfectly preserved colonial city in central Mexico. Located in a narrow canyon between huge mountains where, shortly after its founding in 1559, silver was discovered and the city soon became the richest in Mexico, producing more than a third of the world's silver by the end of the 18th century. Now it is a photographer's delight with plazas, churches, stone steps, cobblestone streets and unique underground passageways. Originally built as drains to prevent flooding, the underground network was converted into a subterranean highway running from one end of the city to the other, alleviating traffic jams on the narrow streets above. Lit at night and surrounded by the foundations of ancient buildings, this sunken road provides an eerie ride unlike any other. The unforgettable result is a centre devoid of traffic lights and neon signs; the topography ensures there is no room for new building.

DTel   **Budget holidays**   14 Feb 23

On a posting to Washington DC, I was advised by another serviceman to take up offers of free accommodation at some wonderful and scenic year-round resorts. We went to one in the Shenandoah Valley in Virginia, another in the Pocono Mountains of Pennsylvania, a third at Daytona Beach, Florida.

We were also entitled to use some family accommodation for US service personnel on a 'space available' basis for much less than elsewhere, using bases in both North and South Carolina and on Governor's Island at the tip of Manhattan. With refundable costs for hotel accommodation while on duty visits, our family of four managed to cover the Eastern seaboard from Bar Harbor, Maine, to Orlando, Florida, by car and at minimum cost over two summer holidays. The only real snag was resisting the pitches trying to sell us timeshares at the resorts - being foreigners with restless children possibly helped.

Daily Telegraph   25 Mar 23
Travel section

Best ever villa holidays

I DID IT MAYA WAY

Our villa on the island of Cozumel, a short ferry ride from Playa del Carmen on the Riviera Maya, was described in the brochure as a mini-hacienda. Its rustic furniture was accentuated with tiles and Mayan wall paintings. Our family of five was happier to socialise here than in a hotel lobby.

There was a pool, a sunbathing area and a thatched *palapa* for those who preferred the shade. We ate in or out, according to our mood, and hired an open-topped VW beetle to explore the island and its beaches. We left reluctantly after a week there, having told the owners that we would be back. Sadly, we just haven't had the chance - yet.

DTel **Calgary** 5 Apr 23

Billed as the Greatest Outdoor Show on Earth, the Calgary Stampede offers the most rambunctious rodeo action anywhere in the world. There can be no sport as daring and dangerous as the Calgary Chuckwagon races which, for the foreign tourist, are best viewed from the magnificent grandstand. But the entertainment does not end when the animals have left the arena; stay for the light-hearted show in the evening. The year I went, a stand-up comedian asked the audience: "What is a Canadian?" The answer, he pronounced, was that "A Canadian is an immigrant with seniority", which received a roar of approval from the crowd. Don't miss it.

A much better letter than mine about Calgary won the letter of the week on 8 Apr 23.

DTel	**Palm Springs**	22 May 23

The sun shines for an average of 350 days a year in Palm Springs and the air is pure. The average daytime temperature is 88°; night-time average, a comfortable 55°. I have been lucky enough to experience two of its most famous features: probably the world's highest number of swimming pools per capita – one for every five people; and its place as 'the Golf Capital of the World'.

My hotel's accommodation led out onto a personal swimming pool; their cars had wooden slats reminiscent of 1950s shooting brakes. By contrast, some of the buggies at the beautifully manicured golf course had miniature Mercedes-Benz or Rolls-Royce radiator grilles; one in coral pink I saw used by a lady golfer had a small television fitted on which she followed a cooking programme during her round.

For anyone, rich or poor, it offers what money cannot buy – a sparkling environment and delightful climate.

Another letter on Palm Springs made the cut.

EXTRAS

Sunday Times   23 Aug 20
Atticus

PM gets a clip-on round the ear (P)*

A debate that strikes at the very heart of the prime minister's personality is raging in The Oldie: has Boris Johnson ever worn a clip-on bow tie?

This deeply wounding (or possibly, quite trivial) allegation was first made when the magazine published a picture of Boris at a 1985 Oxford University ball. In the current issue, reader Malcolm Watson defends the prime minister, insisting that a neckband fastener — not part of a clip-on ensemble — is clearly showing. However, he adds: "Whether Boris Johnson's bow tie . . . is pre-tied or not is another matter altogether."

People can take this sort of thing very seriously. Prince Harry was criticised only last year for wearing a clip-on in public — and now he's fled the country.

*Picture of Prince Harry with an alleged clip-on tie, but actually looking pre-tied. See page 21.

| *The Times*
Feedback | **PM is not married** | 25 Aug 20 |

Dear Rose,

I was surprised to read in yesterday's leading article ("Wish My MP Wasn't There", 24 Aug) that the Prime Minister is married: "… beside the cottage that he and his wife had rented with their infant son… ". I had expected to see a correction published today. Does *The Times* know something that we don't?

Silence.

| *Private Eye* | **Pedantry corner** | 9 Sep 20 |

…Your *Daily Telegraph* extract (p29, Eye 1530) reports that following the Extinction Rebellion disruption of the production of its Saturday edition (5 Sep), their loyal readers "at the weekend were unable to read columns by Allison Pearson, Charles Moore, Nick Timothy and Fraser Nelson". Timothy has a column on Mondays, Pearson on Wednesdays and Nelson on Fridays. I would have got out and collected a copy except that undisrupted I read Charles Moore's Saturday column in the epaper online.

Private Eye	**Commentatorballs**	11 Sep 20

"Really good batting [reverse sweep] - it can go aerial all along the ground.
STUART BROAD, Sky Sport

Private Eye	**Commentatorballs**	2 Oct 20

"It's difficult to circle the square."
MARK MARDELL, BBC Radio 4

The Times *Feedback*	**Young officers**	6 Oct 20

Dear Rose,

Further to my letter, below*, which did not catch the selector's eye, the caption to a picture of Colonel John Waddy (Obituary, Oct 3), also below, shows him "as a young officer in 1958", when he was a major aged 38. In the Army, the term "young officer" is used for subalterns and possibly junior captains, but certainly none of them over 25. It transpires that John Waddy was a major aged 24 at the Battle of Arnhem in 1944, so his time as a "young officer" must have been very short indeed, as it so often must have been in both World Wars.

*See page 28.

The Oldie   **The Jeremy Lewis Prize**   29 Oct 20
for New Writing

In 400 words, recount a memory (similar to the Memory Lane column). Please begin by saying when the events you describe took place.

In April 1970, I was a subaltern in Hong Kong embarked on the commando carrier, HMS *Bulwark*, for a visit to Japan during Expo '70 in Osaka – one leg of what was referred to as "a round-the-world cocktail party". Taken under the wing of the Fleet Air Arm helicopter squadron's officers who awarded two trophies, for being seen in embarrassing situations at each port of call, I was to share a cabin with the latest winner of one of them. The evenings seemed to end with a game involving a nominated drink, a set of dice and some sore heads.

Five days later and following such an evening, the ship was lined for entrance into Kobe harbour. The pilots took pride of place at the bow of the ship and I joined the second rank. Just before coming alongside, an officer in the front rank fell to the deck. He was to win one of the awards on the return journey, not for collapsing, but for his excuse which was that his leg had fallen asleep. Twenty minutes after docking, a Royal Navy mini had been landed on the quay, fitted with Japanese registration plates and four of us were driving along the road - to my surprise - on the left.

So began five unforgettable days at the world exposition and the environs, enjoying activities ranging from admiring the temples and gardens of Kyoto to learning the etiquette of the bathhouse. I well remember a highlight of the fair being a large moon rock on display in the United States' pavilion, brought back by Apollo 12 astronauts in 1969; seeing there the first-ever IMAX film and wondering at demonstrations of early mobile phones, local area networking and magnetic levitation (maglev) train technology.

The return journey to Hong Kong took only four days as the ship shook noisily during speed trials. Passing in the other direction was the accident-prone Australian aircraft carrier HMAS *Melbourne*, at a distance regarded by some of the ship's company as rather too close.

Back in Hong Kong, return hospitality was arranged for my hosts at an officers' mess in the New Territories and from which two large plants were taken as souvenirs. Some weeks later we received a message to say that the plants were well and were "being taken for walkies and wee-wees on the flight deck" - somewhere between Jakarta and Durban.

An abbreviated version, about Expo '70, was published in the Sunday Telegraph Travel section on 17 Jan 21. See page 179.

Sunday Times **Correction** 2 Nov 20

Sir, In the Fame and Fortune piece about Ollie Ollerton (Business, Nov 1), he purports to have told York Membery, in the headline of the screenshot, below, and in main text under "When did you first feel wealthy?", that he was in the army. It was clear from the start of the piece that he was in the Royal Marines and the Special Boat Service, which are part of the Royal Navy and not the army. The error was compounded on page 11 with a link claiming (also below) that "The pay was so bad I left the army". Clearly, he would not have said any such thing.

I suggest that this warrants a published correction.

Dear Mr Watson *4 Nov 20*

Thanks for getting in touch. You are quite correct, of course. The error arose because of a misunderstanding between Mr Ollerton and our interviewer, but it should have been picked up during our checking process. I can only apologise for a poor slip. We have amended our online edition accordingly and a correction will run in print this coming Sunday.

Thank you for pointing this out: it's much appreciated.

Best wishes

Stephen Bleach
Letters editor, The Sunday Times, @stephenbleach

Online, "the army" was replaced with "the forces".

In the print version on 8 Nov 20, the following was published under:

CORRECTIONS & CLARIFICATIONS

Ollie Ollerton did not serve in the army, as we wrongly stated (Money, last week). He served in the Royal Marines and the Special Boat Service, which are parts of the Royal Navy.

The Times **Corrections and clarifications** 30 Nov 20
Feedback

Dear Rose,

On 19 Nov I sent you a copy of my tongue-in-cheek letter to the editor [see page 33]. Since then, the number of corrections and clarifications published in November has risen to a remarkable 23, covering just over 22 column inches - the space roughly taken up by the left- and right-hand columns of the letters page combined. Starting the letters page there every day, I cannot recall such frequency and length of explanations since they first appeared there. Are you able to shed any light onto why this may be happening?

EXTRAS

Patrick Kidd invited readers to email their wittiest suggestions for letters to Santa from famous people (current, historical or fictional,) the best to be printed on Boxing Day.

The Times   15 Dec 20
Diary

Dear Father Christmas,

Please can you bring me another hooded cape, but a size larger than last year. I have not been able to visit my grandmother this year and would like to look my best when I hope I can go to her care home again. I hope you like the Port.

From Little Red Riding Hood

Belated thanks, Malcolm.   *20 Dec 20*
After a slow start I've now received about six times more letters that I will probably have room to use but I shall have a selection meeting on Tuesday and see what I can fit in. I enjoyed this. Patrick

It didn't make it.

The Oldie   **Mrs Kenneth More**   31 Dec 20

Dear Mr Mount,

I was surprised to see you describe Kenneth More's widow as Angela More in your Old Un's Notes in the January issue. Us Old Uns know that she was the actress Angela Douglas and this one, at least, has never seen her referred to by any other name. Now married to producer and director Bill Bryden, she is best remembered for her roles in several *Carry On* films in the 1960s.

As they say in *Private Eye,* maybe I'm the 93rd person to point this out.

The Times   **Corrections and clarifications**   1 Jan 21
Feedback

Dear Rose,

I think that Arthi Nachiappan will find that Ms Sophie Winkleman was listed in court papers as Lady Frederick Windsor and not Lady Sophie Windsor ("Blame the deer, says driver sued over Winkleman crash" News, Jan 1). If not, then she was wrongly named.

Happy New Year to you and your team.

Private Eye   22 Jan 21

Pedantry Corner

...I was surprised to read that a selection panel formed to choose a new chair for the Office of Students (HP Sauce, Eye 1538) included "former peer Baroness Wyld". Only a hereditary peer who has disclaimed their peerage within one year of succeeding to it under the Peerage Act 1963 could possibly be described as being a former peer. Only three peerages are currently disclaimed and Lady Wyld's, being a life peerage, is not one of them. Readers may like to know that she is a former head of the Prime Minister's Appointments Unit, from 2013 to 2016.

Private Eye   **Pseuds Corner**   24 Jan 21

Sir, There must be numerous contenders for inclusion from the world of wine, but I think that this description from Victoria Moore in the *Daily Telegraph* (Jan 23) really takes the biscuit:
"Classic Leyda Valley sauvignon blanc, this wine that smells of white currants and icing sugar, has a

crunchy green feel, as if you're crunching your way through a bowl of mange tout or sugar snaps, with a bit of passion fruit on the side."

Private Eye **Commentatorballs** 1 Feb 21

"Sorry to wind you up."
NICK ROBINSON, Radio 4

Heard to finish an interview of constant interruptions at the end of the Today *programme on Sat 30 Jan 21.*

The Times 27 Feb 21
Feedback column

Harry can feel relieved that he wasn't degraded

Malcolm Watson (Colonel, ret'd) wrote from Ryde on the Isle of Wight, "You reported on your front page that the Duke of Sussex has been stripped of his military duties, but the term 'stripped' has an element of punishment about it. It would have been more accurate — and fairer — to say that he had been 'relieved' of his military duties. This fits with the statement from Buckingham Palace that his military appointments will be returned to Her Majesty."

Fair enough. "Stripped" might well have raised visions of epaulettes being torn from shoulders and swords broken, especially in the context of our photograph, which showed Prince Harry all decked out in medals and gold frogging. I'm not sure, however, if you start to get into the etymology of "relieved of", that it would have been an improvement.

You might be relieved of your responsibilities if you are too sick or overwhelmed to carry them out, but most dictionaries take something like Merriam-Webster's line, where "to relieve of" is defined as "to remove (someone who has done something wrong) from (a post, duty, job, etc). Example: The general was relieved of his command". The other context, of course, in which the expression appears most frequently is when we talk about someone being "relieved of" their wallet, and if you've recently lost your access to the

Sovereign Grant this might have an unpleasantly familiar ring.

Perhaps in the circumstances "stripped" was the better word. At least it made clear that Harry had not given up his military roles voluntarily. There has never been a suggestion that Harry's military record was anything but exemplary, and if he's feeling hard done by at losing the right to wear uniform, he might want to compare the way it happened with the treatment given to Alfred Dreyfus by the French.

In 1894 Captain Dreyfus was falsely accused and convicted of treason by antisemitic fellow officers and sentenced to life imprisonment on Devil's Island. Before being dispatched there he was cashiered, or "degraded", in a ceremony described at length in *The Times*. An adjutant "snatched off the epaulettes, plume, and red stripes of [his] trousers", our reporter noted, going on to sneer that the stitching had been almost completely unpicked in case they were sewn on too tight. "The adjutant," we went on, "concluded by drawing the prisoner's sword from the scabbard, sticking the point in the ground, and breaking it with his foot. The sword had also been previously all but filed off at the spot where it was to be broken."

Last words on the subject from Major General Jeremy Phipps, who prompted the approach: "Well done with the Harry 'stripping' - it got a good airing at least." Jeremy died on 16 March 2021.

Private Eye **Commentatorballs** 21 Mar 21

"…number thirteen, lucky for some…"
ALICE FOX-PITT, ITV Racing

Thirteen is unlucky *for some.*

The Oldie **Not Many Dead** 26 Mar 21

Important stories you may have missed

India and England will play a women's Test sometime in 2021, BCCI announced.
The Cricketer

| *Private Eye* | **Pedantry Corner** | 6 May 21 |

…Re Heir of Sorrows (Eye 1546), what a cacophony of inventive puns - and Huw Jedwards moving from plural to singular - spoilt by the last line. It is HM not HRH Queen Elizabeth the Second… Heads must surely roll.

Many thanks for sending your email. We will be addressing this in the next issue.   *Private Eye*

Another reader got in first.

| *Private Eye* | **Commentatorballs** | 11 Jun 21 |

"They were originally listed in alphabetical order, but obviously that's a bit of an advantage if your company begins with One for example."
CAROLINE DAVIES, BBC News at One

| *Private Eye* | **Pedantry Corner** | 11 Jun 21 |

…If the author is formally known as "Megan, Duchess of Sussex" (The Word of Royalties, Eye 1549) then she is either divorced or widowed. Publishers have pulped their stocks for less. I am staying in to help stamp out this incorrect use of titles.

<table>
<tr><td>*The Times*
Feedback</td><td>**Not approved**</td><td>1 Sep 21</td></tr>
</table>

Dear Rose,

In an effort to pun the phrase 'stamp of approval' the leader writer has wrongly woven in the term approvals ("Stamp of Approval", Aug 31). Stamp collectors do not build up their stocks of "approvals"; they fill gaps in their albums from them. Dealers have stocks from which they make up approvals to send to collectors.

Approvals are priced items sent to meet collectors' needs of frequency, spend and range of items. Collectors choose the items they want and return the rest with payment.

I am sure that the final word of the article - approval - should be preceded with an apostrophe after Gibbons.

I hope this has Rose's approval.

<table>
<tr><td>*The Times*
Feedback</td><td>**Names of regiments**</td><td>17 Oct 21</td></tr>
</table>

Dear Rose,

The Royal Tank Corps became the Royal Tank Regiment in 1939. I always rather hope for better background knowledge from someone described as Defence Editor.

The Times **ECB** 8 Nov 21
Feedback

Dear Rose,

Last week you published two leading articles about
the scandal engulfing Yorkshire County Cricket Club
('Cricket's Shame', Nov 2 & 'Bad Sports', Nov 6). In
both you incorrectly referred to the English Cricket
Board (ECB), when the board is called the England
and Wales Cricket Board, which is indeed abbreviated
to ECB. I had hoped that after the first occasion a
nudge from one of your cricket correspondents would
have prevented the error being repeated. Back in
1997 when the England and Wales Cricket Board
(ECB) came into being, it was always going to be a big
ask for all but devoted followers and commentators
on the game to get it right and so it has proved over
the years. Ironically, if you had used your preferred
style of dropping the capital letters, then the 'english
cricket board (ECB)' could arguably have worked.

As this saga is going to run and run, I do hope that
its correct name can be referred to in future as the
ECB insists on the changes that will be necessary for
Yorkshire to rise once again to the pinnacle of the
county game.   As a member of Yorkshire CCC since
1965 I have more than a passing interest.

Feedback   17 Nov 21

It was good to see the England and Wales Cricket
Board (ECB) correctly referred to in the leading article
"Sporting Failure" (Nov 17).

The Times   **Pupils not children**   9 Dec 21
Feedback

Dear Rose,

Far too often I read of students when what is meant is
pupils, but to describe those awarded top A-level
grades as children cannot be right. In the article "Four
times as many children awarded top A-level grades"
(Dec 9), words used for the cohort range from new
university students, school-leavers, applicants to
university, sixth-formers and 18-year-olds, with the
Department of Education (DfE) using pupils.
Nowhere is children used in the text, so why does it
appear in the title?

The Times   **Correction**   19 Jan 22
Feedback

Dear Rose,

The snippet 'Government wins case' (News, page 4,
Jan 19, below)) starts with: "The government has

overturned a High Court ruling that…". But the government can't overturn a ruling due to the separation of powers. What is meant is that: "The government has had overturned a High Court ruling that…", an important difference which you might consider needs correcting.

| *Sunday Times* | **Grenadier Guards –** | 24 Jan 22 |
| *Complaints* | **Colonels of the Regiment** | |

Sir, I was surprised and disappointed to see your Royal Editor, Roya Nikkhah, writing that the Grenadier Guards has not had a female colonel in its 366-year history (News, Jan 23). The Queen herself, as Princess Elizabeth, was Colonel of the Regiment from 1942 until her accession in 1952, when she became Colonel-in-Chief.

I think a correction would be appropriate.

I expect that I am not the first (or be the last) to point this out.

| *Private Eye* | **Commentatorballs** | 28 Jan 22 |

"You've thrown the gauntlet in their face."
KEN BRUCE, PopMaster, BBC Radio 2

The Times **Please, they are not officers** 24 Mar 22
Feedback

Dear Rose,

I despair at the continued use of the word 'officer' to describe members of the rank and file - or constables and sergeants - of our police forces ("Met hired more than one hundred officers with convictions", News, Mar 23). I imagine that it would be quite exceptional for any members of the Met of officer rank (inspector and upwards) to have a criminal conviction for offences including "handling stolen goods, possession of drugs and assault", or to continue to serve if they acquired one. I accept that "drink-driving" is handled differently. This particular style is one that I believe is not appropriate, especially in this case.

Private Eye 1 Apr 22

Commentatorballs

"All of sudden you've got four or five seconds to make a split-second decision."
JONNY BAIRSTOW, BT Sport

£10 paid for contributions.

The Times   **TMS**   12 Apr 22
Diary

I had ended our brief series on niche museums but Malcolm Watson alerts me to the National Poo Museum on the Isle of Wight, which advertises itself with the slogan: "Have you been?" Malcolm suggests I might like to browse its exhibits but that would surely be going through the motions.
PATRICK KIDD

The series had included the British Lawnmower Museum in Southport; the Derwent pencil museum in Keswick; Barometer World in Merton, Devon; The Centro del Calamar Gigante (giant squid) in Astruas, Spain; Reykyavik's Phallological Museum, with its 200 penises from 46 different species of mammal; the Towing and Recovery Museum in Chattanooga; and the Barbed Wire Museum in La Crosse, Kansas.

The Times
Feedback   **The use of obit and obits**   25 Apr 22

Dear Rose,

I am puzzled in your section on the timing and production of obituaries (Feedback, Apr 23) by the use of the abbreviation 'obit' as both an adjective and a noun, mixed in your text with the word in full. Nigel Farndale's use of the abbreviation throughout his quotes presumably reflects its use as a colloquialism, but I wonder why you use 'obit section', but 'obituaries editor'; 'three obits' but '3000 obituaries'. To quote the correspondent raising the matter: "I imagine that there may be several good reasons…"

The Times
Diary   **TMS**   3 May 22

General Sir Geoffrey Howlett (obituary, Apr 26), who has died at the age of 92, played cricket in a large number of different countries. Not bothered about getting to his half century, this intrepid wandering wicket-keeper was proud of carrying his bat for 49. Anyone played in more?

| *The Times* | **What a wanker** | 5 Jul 22 |
| *Diary* | | |

Patrick,

Haven't times changed for the crowd to be chanting
"Boris is a wanker"? (TMS, 5 June). When a section of
the crowd chanted "Lillie is a wanker" at The Oval
Test in 1975 police moved in and they desisted; until
that is a few minutes later when they opened up
again, but with "Lillie's a self-abuser".

That's quick thinking!
Thanks Malcolm
Patrick

| *The Times* | **Lionesses are heroines** | 2 Aug 22 |
| *Feedback* | | |

Dear Rose,

History has been made - but surely by Lionesses who
are heroines not heroes (The Game, "How gutsy
heroes vanquished German mentality monsters", Aug
1)?
  I note in your style guide: "**actor, actress** for women
use the female designation."

Dear Rose,

You referred to a comment of mine in your column (19 May 2018) that the correct use of Sarah, Duchess of York indicating that she was divorced was "true enough, but…". I was surprised therefore to read yet again of Megan, Duchess of Sussex, but this time in a leading article ("Megan Again", Aug 31). I was even more surprised to read in your Style Guide (2022) that "Widows or former wives of peers who have not remarried use their Christian names before these titles eg. Margaret Duchess of Argyll (no commas) or Mary Lady Jones.

My own particular guide has always been *Titles and Forms of Address, A guide to their correct use*, where the comma is included in such titles. I wonder if *The Times* has created a style of its own to get past the obstacle of not including Christian names where they are not part of the title while meeting the paper's wish to provide them, or whether this new style is acknowledged as now being the correct form and the one with the comma repurposed. I have yet to come across it elsewhere. I think readers would be interested to know. I certainly would.

How I so agree with the thrust of the article though!

| *Private Eye* | **Commentatorballs** | 4 Sep 22 |

"She hit that so late, she hit that yesterday."
MARTINA NAVRATILOVA, Amazon Prime

| *The Times* Feedback | **Great offices of state** | 20 Oct 22 |

Dear Rose,

Oliver Wright, policy editor, writes that: "Four out of five of the great offices of state are now made up of MPs who opposed Brexit in 2016" ("The only allies left wield a mean stiletto", News Politics, Oct 20). But it is generally recognised elsewhere that there are four such offices of state: prime minister, chancellor of the exchequer, foreign secretary and home secretary. I wrote pointing this out on May 2 2019 when a leading article that day wrongly had the defence secretary as a (fifth) great office of state. A quick search shows that Patrick Maguire knows there are four viz: "Two out of four of the great offices of state are occupied by women for only the second time . . .", (Red Box, Sep 16 2021). Could this myth about a fifth great office of state be corrected at *The Times*?

DTel **Trainers in the House of Lords** 8 Nov 22
Peterborough column

Dear Mr Hope,

I was surprised to find you choosing a pen used by
Lord Soames of Fletching - without photographic
evidence - to question whether standards are slipping
in the House of Lords, when the paper published a
photograph of the now noble lord wearing trainers
that illustrated the point exactly (News, page 2,
November 1). I do hope that he had a proper pair of
polished black leather shoes to change into once
inside the building.

DTel **Lady Swire** 15 Nov 22
Peterborough column

Dear Mr Hope,

Hugo Swire's wife has been Lady Swire since her
husband was knighted in David Cameron's
Resignation Honours in 2016. Some wind up by Boris
Johnson then (Peterborough, November 12)! Is there
no hope?

| *The Times* | **The moderator** | 18 Nov 22 |
| *Feedback* | | |

Dear Rose,

Buoyed by the publication of my letter on Wednesday and its airing on Times Radio the following day, I am geared up to write to you once more; in fact, on 3 different matters which I will address in separate emails for (I hope) ease of handling your end.

First, below the article "Prince Andrew thought it was all over" (Nov 11/12), with a comment attracting 760 recommendations, you will see the word "s hit" in the first line. In response I posted a comment along the lines of "I wonder if by placing a space in the word 's hit' this has got around the moderator?" You will see on the screenshot below that it was my comment that appears to have violated your policy and not the subject of the comment. Can this really be right?

| *The Times* | **Lady Susan Hussey** | 10 Dec 22 |
| *Feedback* | | |

Dear Rose,

It is reassuring to know that I am not the only one who is a stickler for correctness (feedback, Dec 10)! You say that Lady Susan Hussey has chosen to stay with that style and that you are happy to conform. Unfortunately, you didn't: in the leading article ("Royal Reason", Dec 2), 'Lady Susan Hussey' changes to 'Lady Hussey' in the second paragraph (screenshot below), when 'Lady Susan', as you have used yourself, would have been appropriate if a shortened form was needed. Are leader writers and subs now too young to have watched *Downton Abbey*? Also, 'Susan Hussey' is surely too familiar to have been used above the main text (or just plain wrong)?

The Times	**Ladies' titles - again**	10 Dec 22
Feedback		

Dear Rose,

I had hoped to get some feedback to my email of 2 Sep 22, below, but seem to remember that it was sent during one of those periods that you were away. I return to the content following publication of your obituary of Belinda, Lady Montagu of Beaulieu (Dec 19), in which the comma is used in her title contrary to your apparent preferred style (see below highlighted in yellow), but correctly in my view. And yet, in the third paragraph from the end Sophie, Countess of Wessex is used when she is neither divorced nor widowed. Surely they can't both be right?

The Cricketer magazine asked readers to nominate, up to three, of their favourite cricket books Here are my nominations.

Dear Huw,   22 Feb 23

A test of the esteem in which a book is held is surely obtaining another copy when it has been lost. This was the fate of my paperback version of Ramachandra Guha's *A Corner of a Foreign Field* (2003). Its content and pedigree are acknowledged in the magazine's June 2020 feature, with only *The Art of Captaincy* getting more mentions and *Larwood* the same number. Strangely, it took some years to find a replacement at a sensible price, but I will not be lending it again.

Another test is what to keep out when all but a handful of your books have to go into storage. Peter Wynne Thomas's *The Complete History of Cricket Tours at Home and Abroad* (1989) twice came across the Atlantic Ocean for postings to Washington DC and Mexico City. It is an invaluable reference volume covering 1859 to 1988 with the background to the tours, photos of teams or touring parties, some next to ships' gangways or passenger aircraft steps, results and averages. The author did not produce an updated version due to the proliferation of subsequent tours.

My third choice - which also meets the tests for the first two - is *Sweet Summers: The Classic Writing of J.M. Kilburn* edited by Duncan Hamilton. This collection of essays, reports and vignettes of great players is best described with the words completing its nomination as the *Wisden* Book of the Year in 2009: "…his work deserves to be read for as long as cricket is played." Should you find my selection of any use I can probably cut the wordage to what you might have space for!

The sheer range of books we have had, Malcolm.
I have filled up 2 sides of A4 and only about a handful have more than 1 vote.
Thanks and best wishes, Huw

| *The Times* | **Bettys' apostrophes** | **23** Feb 23 |
| *Feedback* | | |

Dear Rose,

I was amused to read the correspondence (letters, Feb 17 and 23) following Janice Turner's notebook entry about "Betty's" café (and tried to enter it myself, below), *however*, the apostrophe was dropped from the name in 1965. Interestingly, a fictional version of the café appeared in the *Downton Abbey* series (2014) based in 1924 had the apostrophe removed decades before the rebrand. This explanation was provided through the Northern Echo:

"In the 1920s Bettys was spelled with an apostrophe - but we chose to leave it out in our fictional Downton

tea room signage so that anyone who spotted us
would recognise us.

"We also took some further artistic licence and
included Fat Rascals in the window – they weren't yet
invented in 1924, but who would know Bettys
without a Fat Rascal in the window?"

Not Janice Turner or Dr Roger Norwich (letter, Feb
23) anyway!

*The italics in the first sentence refer to Rose's column on
the Saturday where she had declared that* however *was the
most dreaded word in the Feedback mailbox.*

Sunday Times   **February 19 edition**   26 Feb 23
Complaints
Copies to:
Sport, Culture letters

Sir,

1. <u>Sport</u>. Someone cobbled together the headline
beginning "English cricket and sport is…" on the back
page on Feb 19. It wouldn't have been Ed Smith*.

2. <u>Culture</u>. On page 47, the caption below a picture of
German naval officers includes: "plotting the
destruction of Nazi submarines". I don't somehow
think they would be hoping to destroy their own.

Ed Smith, who wrote the article, has a double first from Cambridge.

Private *Eye* **Commentatorballs** 4 Mar 23

"We're off for a pint. Just a quick half."
JORDAN NORTH, ITV1

The Times **Port consumption** 8 Mar 23
TMS

I was interested to read in TMS today that William Wilberforce cut his drinking down to only six glasses of port a day. You may be equally interested to know that Alfred, Lord Tennyson's consumption exceeded that. The story told at Farringford, his home in the Isle of Wight, is: "The novelist Henry James noted that Tennyson would drink a whole bottle of port at one sitting and he did this almost nightly even into old age." That would be 10 glasses a day, though a quick look at the first and last verses of the poem The Cock indicates that this could well have been done using a pint-pot.

I wonder if port helps to promote beard growth... He certainly had wonderful whiskers. Maybe it was less strong in those days. And did he have a cheeseboard with it?
    Good to hear from you.
Patrick

Private Eye   **Pedantry Corner**   25 Mar 23

…You report that magnet fishing in the Baltimore area has become a craze in recent months ('Funny Old World', Eye 1593) and that all sorts of things have been pulled from the harbour, including scooters, chairs and even a gun. The drawing illustrating a bundle being raised from the water has the haul coloured yellow, like brass or even gold. However, brass and gold are non-magnetic and the magnet would not attach to the bundle. Also, the rope would need to be in tension to raise even an empty magnet. Just saying…

DTel   **Corrections of letters**   26 Apr 23
Letters Editor

Dear Orlando [Bird],

You have published today two letters (from Towyn Evans and Geraldine Pickthall) in which they talk about British embassies in Kenya and Papua New Guinea. Being members of the Commonwealth, we have British High Commissions in those countries not embassies.

Isn't one of the reasons that we have to include a telephone number when submitting letters for publication, so that your staff can contact the writer and correct such errors, or are your team unaware of this distinction about our representation abroad?

Dear Malcolm   *26 Apr 23*

Many thanks for alerting me to that - a shaming lapse! At least it's now correct online. Must try harder.

All the best

Orlando

EVEN MORE
LAST WORDS

"To be really happy and really safe,
one ought to have at least two or three
hobbies and they must all be real."

Sir Winston Churchill (1874-1965)

ACKNOWLEDGEMENTS

This book has been self-published, which as the term implies, you have to do it yourself and that is what I have done for the fifth time, using lulu.com as a development tool, but Amazon's Kindle Direct Publishing for the second time for publication.

However, special thanks are due to Michael Bromley Gardner, whose eagle eye has become indispensable for spotting typos and errors.

I am also indebted to three more acknowledged exponents of the written word in their respective fields for their enticing forewords and to another, Hunter Davies, the author, journalist and broadcaster for his supportive endorsement on the back cover.

Finally, to the late Bill Tidy, for his fourth cartoon for the front cover and his continued enthusiasm for a joint project, though it didn't in the end materialise.

ABOUT THE SUBJECT

Malcolm Watson was born in Beverley in the East Riding of Yorkshire and educated at Oundle and the Royal Military Academy Sandhurst, being commissioned into The Queen's Own Hussars; and at the Royal Military College of Science Shrivenham, from where he obtained a degree in Aeromechanical Engineering. He was in the Army for 39 years, serving at various times in England and Northern Ireland, and abroad in Cyprus, Hong Kong, West Germany, West Berlin, Washington DC and Mexico City, where as the defence attaché he was also accredited to Belize and Cuba. He has made 10 military parachute jumps and flown 40 hours in a Piper Cherokee. He played and watched more cricket than was thought possible for a serviceman; he has been a member of Yorkshire County Cricket Club since 1965 and MCC since 1980. He enjoys acting the fool and has taken part in a number of revues on stage and elsewhere. His only serious and non-speaking part, to date, was playing King George IV at his Coronation in the Berlin Military Tattoo. He is interested in everything except classical music, Shakespeare and Greek mythology. He is married to Jane and they have 3 daughters, Anna, Edwina and Fenella.

"…he will speak his mind whenever the occasion warrants it (and perhaps some when it does not!)…"
Extract from a Regular Army Confidential Report

WHAT THEY SAID ABOUT

The Wit and Wisdom of an Ordinary Subject
(2013)

"Most interesting."
Sir Max Hastings

More Wit and Wisdom of an Ordinary Subject
(2014)

"I salute a fellow practitioner of
the epistolary arts."
Lord Lexden

*Yet More Wit and Wisdom of an Ordinary
Subject* (2016)

"A delightful mix of the witty, whimsical,
perceptive and downright serious."
Martin Johnson, Sports columnist

*Much More Wit and Wisdom of an Ordinary
Subject* (2020)

"In terms of letter writing to both newspapers
and magazines, he is truly a great man of letters."
Mark Hedges, Editor, *Country Life*

Printed in Great Britain
by Amazon

26126470R00143